CAPM® Exam Success Series:
Exam Simulation Booklet

Crosswind
Project Management Inc.
www.crosswindpm.com

Copyright Page

CAPM® Exam Success Series: Exam Simulation Booklet

Tony Johnson. – 2nd ed.

p.cm.

ISBN: 978-1-935062-15-8

Johnson, Tony 2. CAPM 3. CAPM Certification 4. Project Management I. Title

Thank you for choosing this book. We hope your experience with it was as satisfying for you as it was for us to create.

-- Team Crosswind

Disclaimer

Every attempt has been made by the publisher and author to have the contents of this book provide accurate information for the reader to pass the PMP® (Project Management Professional) Examination. The publisher and author, however accept no legal responsibility for the contents therein. The opinions of the author in this book do not necessarily reflect that of PMI (Project Management Institute).

Both the publisher and author of this book warn readers to use not just this book, but at the very least also the *PMBOK* (Project Management Body of Knowledge) Guide in their attempts to pass the CAPM (Certified Associate Project Management) exam to become CAPM-certified. The publisher and the author also acknowledge that the purchase of this book does not guarantee that the reader will pass the CAPM (Certified Associate Project Management) exam. Neither the author nor the publisher will be held liable for individuals who do not heed to this warning.

"CAPM" is a registered certification mark of the Project Management Institute, Inc.

PMI does not endorse or otherwise Sponsor this publication and makes no warranty, guarantee, or representation, expressed or implied, as to its accuracy or content.

If you discover what you believe to be an error in this book, please check our Web site www.crosswindpm.com for errata that has been discovered. If you don't see the item under the question listed, email the page, WBS#, and details to info@crosswindpm.com.

Trademarks and Copyrights

Throughout this manual, we reference and recognize the following trademarks, service marks, and copyrights of Project Management Institute (PMI):

PMP®

PMP® Certification

PMP® Exam

PMI®

PMBOK®

CAPM®

CAPM® Certification

CAPM® Exam

PgMP®

Dedication

To the people who practice the science of Project Management every day with a passion for excellence and doing things the right way. You are the people who remember that we are growing an industry and profession with Project Management, not just passing a test.

Thanks

Team is a very important piece of the Crosswind culture. From our alumni network of evangelists to the Crosswind staff, to the team of people who contributed in various ways to what you are about to read in this book.

The following played a key role with their contributions:

Sergio, Analaura, Ramya, Bill: Thank you for helping build the foundation to help us become the success we are today.

Denise, Jessica, Richard, Aaron, Aaron (2), Reanna, Sana, Michael, Jeff, Nordy, Mike, Danny, and Aly: Focusing on product development and keeping things running each day as well. We aren't the same without you.

Brian, Kevin, Ramya, Rachel, Boriana, Mythili, Tim, Venkat, Angie, Bob, Jessica, Soumya, Rebecca, and Joyce: The QC team of the decade…Your commitment to our products and our customers is unparalleled.

Brett, Beverly, Shelley, Chris, AJ, Shari and Lynda: Thank you for your creativity and dedication to quality. Crosswind took it to the next level when you joined the team.

Paul, Sherri, Adam, and Hal….when it's hammer time you are there keeping the foundation strong…

Addison Road: You know the three words……You do it well!

Tom, your passion and growth of Project management to make PM and our book all they can be

The Houston PMI® Chapter: Andy Stuart, Kathy Ridley, Marc DeCantillon, your support is much appreciated!

The Dallas and Fort Worth PMI® Chapters: Past Presidents John C. Baley, and Jonathan Overton; Current Presidents Dwaraka Iyengar and Dick Walz; and Fort Worth VPs of Education Matthew Solodow and Sandy Harris, for your support!

The Crosswind Evangelist (Alumni) Network: For your never-ending desire to learn and keep me moving!

Sam and the staff at TP on I-35 in Lewisville, review and editing is a whole new environment with you…

About Crosswind Project Management, Inc.

Crosswind Project Management, Inc. started in 1998 to serve the needs of various technical customers in the Dallas/Fort Worth, Texas area. As the company evolved, it stepped into the education and training arena in the local junior colleges and began to grow its curriculum while helping make a difference in people's lives and careers.

As the dotcom and telecom economies were at their peak, Crosswind was offering PMP Certification training to companies in the Dallas area, as well as the southern United States. All the while, the PMP and CAPM Exam Success Series was being developed and fine-tuned.

Today, Crosswind Project Management's CAPM Exam Success Series of products are some of the most integrated and efficient products on the market for CAPM Certification. They are currently used in numerous industries and in various universities, colleges, and PMI chapters in at least 43 countries.

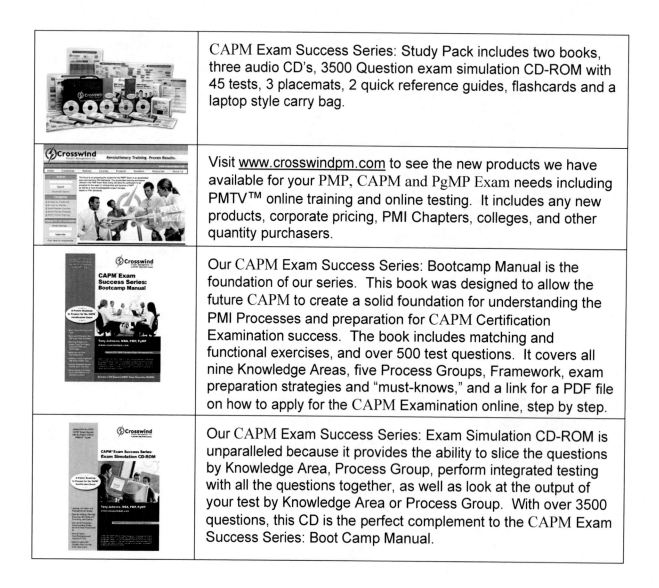

	CAPM Exam Success Series: Study Pack includes two books, three audio CD's, 3500 Question exam simulation CD-ROM with 45 tests, 3 placemats, 2 quick reference guides, flashcards and a laptop style carry bag.
	Visit www.crosswindpm.com to see the new products we have available for your PMP, CAPM and PgMP Exam needs including PMTV™ online training and online testing. It includes any new products, corporate pricing, PMI Chapters, colleges, and other quantity purchasers.
	Our CAPM Exam Success Series: Bootcamp Manual is the foundation of our series. This book was designed to allow the future CAPM to create a solid foundation for understanding the PMI Processes and preparation for CAPM Certification Examination success. The book includes matching and functional exercises, and over 500 test questions. It covers all nine Knowledge Areas, five Process Groups, Framework, exam preparation strategies and "must-knows," and a link for a PDF file on how to apply for the CAPM Examination online, step by step.
	Our CAPM Exam Success Series: Exam Simulation CD-ROM is unparalleled because it provides the ability to slice the questions by Knowledge Area, Process Group, perform integrated testing with all the questions together, as well as look at the output of your test by Knowledge Area or Process Group. With over 3500 questions, this CD is the perfect complement to the CAPM Exam Success Series: Boot Camp Manual.

	The CAPM Exam Success Series: Exam Questions Book is a manual full of CAPM Examination questions different from our Certification Exam Manual. Each question has a full explanation to help reinforce learning.
	The CAPM Exam Success Series: Processes, ITTO's, and Mindmaps placemats provide a summary to the point of view of the information needed for the CAPM Examination. Processes, Inputs, Tools and Techniques Outputs, Plans, Formulas, Mind Maps, and other key pieces are all there. A double-sided, laminated 11" X 17" card provides you the key to CAPM for the exam and a long-term quick reference after you are a CAPM.
	The CAPM Exam Success Series: Understanding the Processes and CAPM Exam Success Series: Terms and Definitions audio CDs are ideal for that late night listening or carpool study time. Designed to complement the rest of the CAPM Success Series, this audio part of the process helps reinforce your development. Each CD contains 80 minutes of information professionally recorded to help get you ready for the CAPM Examination.
	The CAPM Exam Success Series: Certification Exam Flashcards are the key tool for working through lunch studying the 400+ terms, definitions, key inputs, key tools and key outputs, formulas, and variables. It helps reinforce the learning and understanding of all 42 processes and their associated pieces.

Also, please let us know of your success with becoming a CAPM®. Email info@crosswindpm.com to tell us what we did that worked for you. Your feedback helps us evolve our products to make them the most advanced, cutting edge products on the market today!

PMTV™ Online PMP/CAPM Examination Review
PMTV's free online Tip of the Day and PMP/CAPM Examination Review is available. Visit www.crosswindpm.com to sign up for automated Tip of the Day updates. You will receive updates plus information on the complementary trial account.

Online Examination Review
As this book went to press, development of the online Examination Review was ongoing. Visit www.crosswindpm.com to sign up for automated training course updates. You will receive updates as the product launches plus information on the complementary trial account.

About the Author

Tony Johnson, MBA, PMP, PgMP, has over 18 years experience as a Project Manager in industries such as telecommunications, finance, consulting, hardware and software development, education, and manufacturing.

He has multiple years of experience in training and curriculum development plus training in areas such as technology, manufacturing, Internet, electronic commerce, and project management. He has delivered over 9000 hours of project management training in alignment with PMI Standards.

He has contributed toward the most recently released PMI Standards. Specifically he has contributed toward the *PMBOK*® Guide – Fourth Edition, the Standard for Program Management – Second Edition, the Standard for Portfolio Management – Second Edition, and the OPM3 Knowledge Foundation – Second Edition.

Former students come from companies such as:

AAFES	Accenture	ACS	Adea Solutions	Auto One
American Airlines	Anderson Consulting	AT&T	Avaya	Bank of America
Bank One	Bearing Point	Carreker	Ciber	Cisco
Cingular	Citi	CompUSA	Computer Associates	Crossmark
PMI Dallas Chapter Education Committee	Decision Consultants, Inc.	Department of Defense	Electronic Data Systems (EDS)	Excel Communications
Exe	Fujitsu	Harley-Davidson	Hewlett-Packard	Honeywell
IBM	Immedient	Intellimark-IT	Interstate Battery	JCPenney
Lucent	Genuity	KPMG	Macromedia	Match.com
MCI	Motorola	Nortel	Oracle	Perot Systems
PWC	Sabre	Source	Southwestern Bell Corporation	Technisource
Texas Instruments	Travelocity	Tyco	U.S. Air Force	Vartec
Verizon	U.S. Army	U.S. Navy	Wal-Mart	Worldcom

Mr. Johnson is also an award-winning member of the Dallas PMI chapter (one of the world's largest chapters with over 4000 members, 67% of whom are PMPs), as well as a past member of the chapter's education committee. He has also been a key presenter at the chapter's PMP Forum and chapter meetings.

Mr. Johnson has a bachelor's degree in Business Administration and Finance from Dallas Baptist University and an MBA in Operations and Strategic Management from Dallas Baptist University. He has taught at Southern Methodist University (SMU), as well as various colleges and universities in Dallas, Texas. He is the founder of Crosswind Project Management Inc. (www.crosswindpm.com).

Table of Contents

Answer Sheets

We recommend that you make multiple photocopies of the answer sheets so you can practice the test as many times as you like.

Knowledge Area Answer Sheet

Topic Name:	Date:
1.	16.
2.	17.
3.	18.
4.	19.
5.	20.
6.	21.
7.	22.
8.	23.
9.	24.
10.	25.
11.	26.
12.	27.
13.	28.
14.	29.
15.	30.

CAPM® Exam Simulation Booklet
© 2008 Crosswind Project Management Inc, www.crosswindpm.com

Full CAPM® Exam Simulation Answer Sheet

Date:		Start Time:		
		Stop Time:		
1.	31.	61.	91.	121.
2.	32.	62.	92.	122.
3.	33.	63.	93.	123.
4.	34.	64.	94.	124.
5.	35.	65.	95.	125.
6.	36.	66.	96.	126.
7.	37.	67.	97.	127.
8.	38.	68.	98.	128.
9.	39.	69.	99.	129.
10.	40.	70.	100.	130.
11.	41.	71.	101.	131.
12.	42.	72.	102.	132.
13.	43.	73.	103.	133.
14.	44.	74.	104.	134.
15.	45.	75.	105.	135.
16.	46.	76.	106.	136.
17.	47.	77.	107.	137.
18.	48.	78.	108.	138.
19.	49.	79.	109.	139.
20.	50.	80.	110.	140.
21.	51.	81.	111.	141.
22.	52.	82.	112.	142.
23.	53.	83.	113.	143.
24.	54.	84.	114.	144.
25.	55.	85.	115.	145.
26.	56.	86.	116.	146.
27.	57.	87.	117.	147.
28.	58.	88.	118.	148.
29.	59.	89.	119.	149.
30.	60.	90.	120.	150.

Framework

1. What will the project team create as a result of performing monitoring and controlling on a project?

    (A) Charter
    (B) Controlling Stakeholders
    (C) Corrective Action
    (D) Project product

2. You are brought into a planning meeting by senior management at your company. They inform you that you have been selected to be the Project Manager for a new project that will help the company acquire a new company that will fill a market need they have been trying to fill for five years. This project is the result of what type of planning?

    (A) Program planning
    (B) Portfolio planning
    (C) Product Life Cycle
    (D) Strategic planning

3. On a banking system project, the team is large and communication has been out of control. The Project Expeditor has been used to help with this problem. What is one of the main differences between the Project Expeditor and Project Coordinator?

    (A) The Project Expeditor is another title for the Project Manager
    (B) The Project Expeditor is another title for Project Coordinator
    (C) The Project Expeditor has limited or no decision-making ability
    (D) The Project Expeditor has decision-making ability

4. Two people at work are discussing roles and responsibilities as they relate to the company and the projects it has. They are discussing the role of the Project Manager and the functional manager. What is the main role of the functional manager?

    (A) To control resources
    (B) To manage the project when the Project Manager isn't available
    (C) To define business processes
    (D) To manage the Project Managers

5. What are the five process groups used in the *PMBOK®* Guide?

    (A) Requirements, System Development, Testing, UAT
    (B) Initiating, Planning Executing, Testing, Closure
    (C) Initiating, Planning, Executing, Monitoring and Controlling, Closing
    (D) Initiating, Planning, Executing, Testing, Signoff

6. When the initiating process is complete, what will be created?

    (A) Work results
    (B) Charter
    (C) A signed contract
    (D) Corrective action

7. Which of the following best describes a Project Manager's position on change on a project?

    (A) To control unnecessary change
    (B) To delay changes so the project can be completed
    (C) Expedite all Change Requests to the Change Control Board
    (D) Protect the Change Control Board from seeing any more change than they need to

8. Which of the following is the most important job for the Project Manager on a global infrastructure upgrade project?

    (A) Controlling unnecessary change
    (B) Exceeding customer expectations
    (C) Creating the project management plan
    (D) Controlling Stakeholders

9. In creating the project management plan for a construction project, a team would typically be involved in creating all the following except…

    (A) Budget
    (B) Risk Management Plan
    (C) Schedule
    (D) Information Distribution Plan

10. On a large scale global technology upgrade project, who is responsible for creating and executing the project management plan?

    (A) The company that was awarded the outsourcing contract
    (B) The Project Manager
    (C) The Project Manager and the team
    (D) The team

11. In considering the triple constraint for a project, which of the following would the team find of most importance?

    (A) Time then Scope then Cost
    (B) Quality then Time then Cost
    (C) Scope
    (D) They are all of equal importance unless otherwise stated

12. The functional manager is working on planning the data center project with the newest Project Manager at the company. In discussing this, the functional manager is focusing on the costs associated with running the data center after it is created, and for how many years the data center will be used. What best describes what the functional manager is focusing on?

    (A) Project life cycle
    (B) Product life cycle
    (C) Project management life cycle
    (D) Program management life cycle

13. A construction project has just completed the initiation process. Planning is ready to begin. Which of the following have the project team just completed and which are they ready to start?

    (A) The project management plan and project execution
    (B) The charter and project planning
    (C) The project execution and monitoring and controlling
    (D) The charter and project execution

14. What is the main deliverable from the planning phase of a project?

    (A) Project management plan
    (B) A signed contract
    (C) Charter
    (D) Work results

15. The team of Project Managers works in a company with a variety of projects. Typically, they are involved in assigning Project Managers, and creating and maintaining documentation and policies. What is the name of the place where they work?

    (A) Tight Matrixed
    (B) Project Management Office
    (C) Projectized
    (D) Functional

16. All the following are regulations except…

    (A) The average speed on a street in a day
    (B) The zoning for an area
    (C) The building code for a city
    (D) The documented way to dispose of old computers

17. Which of the following environments would make the best use of cross-functional work teams?

    (A) An offshore company
    (B) A data warehouse practice
    (C) Union-approved workplaces
    (D) A project that utilizes all groups across a company

18. What will the development team have created as a result of completing the work of the project?

    (A) Charter
    (B) Work results
    (C) Project product
    (D) A signed contract

19. The data warehouse project is reorganized to reflect a projectized structure. Which of the following would be considered an advantage for the team members?

    (A) Optimization for a single focus on the project
    (B) Business unit competency
    (C) A place to go when the project is complete
    (D) Having to get approval from Functional Management

20. The project team is in the process of setting expectations with the stakeholders on the project. Which of the following best describes a stakeholder?

    (A) The Project Manager
    (B) A team member
    (C) All the answers
    (D) Someone who works in an area impacted by the work of the project

21. If the team is in the process of updating a schedule on a project with actuals from the project, which of the following would they use?

    (A) Schedule Management Plan
    (B) Control Schedule
    (C) Time Management Plan
    (D) Work Breakdown Structure

22. A business analyst has a career path that has been very important to her throughout the twelve years of her career. She is put on a project with a projectized structure. Which of the following is likely viewed as a negative of being on the project?

    (A) Working with people who have similar skills
    (B) Not being able to take the BAP certification test because she will be so busy
    (C) Working long hours because the project is a high priority
    (D) Being away from the group and on a project that might make it more difficult to get promoted

23. In a travel agency upgrade project, the Project Manager has been extremely busy. Senior management has begun to become more involved. What is the typical role of Senior Management on a project?

    (A) Pays for it
    (B) Support the project
    (C) Resolves resource and other conflicts
    (D) Supports the project and resolves resource and other conflict

24. The point of sale project is 75% complete at a major retail client. Your company is doing the implementation and has twenty three team members in various locations across five different buildings. Communication and team-building has been a real challenge. Which of the following would fix or improve this problem?

    (A) Replacing the Project Manager
    (B) Hiring Project Coordinators
    (C) Changing the organization to a functional structure
    (D) Co-location

25. Which of the following is considered an advantage of a Functional Organization if you are an accountant?

    (A) Not having a home when the project is complete
    (B) Having a home to go to when the project is complete
    (C) Having more than one boss
    (D) Having more than one project to work on

26. The project management life cycle is most similar to which of the following?

    (A) SDLC
    (B) Project life cycle
    (C) Use case analysis
    (D) Plan-Do-Check-Act

27. The project management team is focusing on the Project Management Life Cycle and the Project Life Cycle. What is the main difference between these two?

    (A) The Project Management Life Cycle is done in the project and the Project Life Cycle is done after the project is complete.
    (B) The Project Management Life Cycle is the process of completing the work of the project and the Project Life Cycle is the Project Management piece of the project.
    (C) They are the same.
    (D) The Project Management Life Cycle is the Project Management piece of the project and the Project Life Cycle is the process of completing the work of the project.

28. In project management, there are a number of key roles associated with project success. Which role would the Project Manager work with for more funding on the project and involve in the signoff process?

    (A) The stockholders
    (B) The Project Manager
    (C) The department manager
    (D) The Sponsor

29. Which of the following is an example of a standard?

    (A) The number of slides in your last presentation
    (B) The average speed that someone drives to work
    (C) The shade of paint selected to paint your office
    (D) 700MB capacity for a CD-ROM.

30. Which of the following best describes utilizing program management across an organization?

(A) Managing of related or similar projects in a coordinated way
(B) The process of computer program management
(C) Managing a television program
(D) Done for a purpose

Framework Answer Key

1. What will the project team create as a result of performing monitoring and controlling on a project?

    Correct Answer: (C) Corrective Action
    Explanation: Corrective Action is the main output of Monitoring and Controlling. The Charter comes from initiation. The project product comes from Closing. Controlling Stakeholders is noise.

2. You are brought into a planning meeting by senior management at your company. They inform you that you have been selected to be the Project Manager for a new project that will help the company acquire a new company that will fill a market need they have been trying to fill for five years. This project is the result of what type of planning?

    Correct Answer: (D) Strategic planning
    Explanation: Strategic planning is a type of planning that is typically done three to five years in advance. It is very common for projects to be driven by strategic initiative at a company. Product life cycle involves the entire life cycle from "cradle to grave" for a product. The other two answers are noise.

3. On a banking system project, the team is large and communication has been out of control. The Project Expeditor has been used to help with this problem. What is one of the main differences between the Project Expeditor and Project Coordinator?

    Correct Answer: (C) The Project Expeditor has limited or no decision-making ability
    Explanation: The Project Expeditor and Project Coordinator have similar responsibilities with the difference being that the Project Coordinator has some decision-making ability.

4. Two people at work are discussing roles and responsibilities as they relate to the company and the projects it has. They are discussing the role of the Project Manager and the functional manager. What is the main role of the functional manager?

    Correct Answer: (A) To control resources
    Explanation: The functional manager runs the day-to-day business and is responsible for resources. Project Managers do not always report to functional managers. The functional manager, not the Project Manager, runs a department or area of business. Defining business processes is noise.

5. What are the five process groups used in the *PMBOK®* Guide?

    Correct Answer: (C) Initiating, Planning, Executing, Monitoring and Controlling, Closing
    Explanation: Per the *PMBOK®* Guide - Fourth Edition, the process groups that make up the PMI methodology or "Project Management Life Cycle" are Initiating, Planning, Executing, Monitoring and Controlling, and Closing.

6. When the initiating process is complete, what will be created?

    Correct Answer: (B) Charter
    Explanation: The main output of initiating is the Charter. Work results come from project execution. Corrective action comes from Controlling. A signed contract is noise.

7.   Which of the following best describes a Project Manager's position on change on a project?

Correct Answer: (A) To control unnecessary change
Explanation: The main job of a Project Manager, other than managing the project itself, is to control unnecessary change that can derail the project. Delaying changes and protecting the Change Control Board (CCB) from changes are both unprofessional. Expediting changes to the CCB is not a bad answer but not the best.

8.   Which of the following is the most important job for the Project Manager on a global infrastructure upgrade project?

Correct Answer: (A) Controlling unnecessary change
Explanation: Controlling unnecessary change is one of the biggest challenges for Project Managers to do well. If they don't do this well, the project can go out of control. Creating the project management plan is a good answer, but if changes are out of control, the best plan won't do any good. Exceeding customer expectations is unnecessary and could likely result in Gold Plating which isn't good. Controlling Stakeholders is noise.

9.   In creating the project management plan for a construction project, a team would typically be involved in creating all the following except…

Correct Answer: (D) Information Distribution Plan
Explanation: The budget, schedule, and risk management plan are parts of the project management plan as they deal with the time, money, and risk parts of the project. Information Distribution Plan is noise

10.   On a large scale global technology upgrade project, who is responsible for creating and executing the project management plan?

Correct Answer: (B) The Project Manager
Explanation: The Project Manager is responsible for creating the project management plan. This creation typically comes with the help of the team. The Project Manager is responsible for execution of the plan and the team members are responsible for the plan's activities. The outsourcing answer is noise.

11.   In considering the triple constraint for a project, which of the following would the team find of most importance?

Correct Answer: (D) They are all of equal importance unless otherwise stated
Explanation: The Triple Constraint of Project Management is that Scope, Time, and Cost are all equal unless otherwise defined as such. Quality is often confused in place of Scope with the Triple Constraint. Quality is actually achieved when Scope, Time, and Cost goals have been met.

12.   The functional manager is working on planning the data center project with the newest Project Manager at the company. In discussing this, the functional manager is focusing on the costs associated with running the data center after it is created, and for how many years the data center will be used. What best describes what the functional manager is focusing on?

Correct Answer: (B) Product life cycle
Explanation: The product life cycle focuses on the overall ownership costs of the product of the project, not just the project costs to create the product. The project life cycle involves the processes used to create the product of the project such as the steps to build a house or a computer system. The project management life cycle is the project management approach to the project. The program management life cycle is noise.

13. A construction project has just completed the initiation process. Planning is ready to begin. Which of the following have the project team just completed and which are they ready to start?

    Correct Answer: (B) The charter and project planning
    Explanation: The Project Management Life Cycle is Initiating, Planning, Executing, Monitoring and Controlling, and Closing. The main output of initiation is the creation of a Charter. Once this is done, the creation of the project management plan can start. The other answers are either out of sync with the life cycle or are noise.

14. What is the main deliverable from the planning phase of a project?

    Correct Answer: (A) Project management plan
    Explanation: The main output of Planning is the project management plan. The Charter comes from Initiation. Work results come from project execution. A signed contract is noise.

15. The team of Project Managers works in a company with a variety of projects. Typically, they are involved in assigning Project Managers, and creating and maintaining documentation and policies. What is the name of the place where they work?

    Correct Answer: (B) Project Management Office
    Explanation: The Project Management Office (PMO) can control Project Managers, documentation and policies or anything else needed within reason for the management of projects within an organization. The functional organization is more of a business unit structure such as marketing. Projectized would focus only on completion of a project or project. Tight Matrixed is noise.

16. All the following are regulations except…

    Correct Answer: (A) The average speed on a street in a day
    Explanation: The average speed on a street in a day is simply a value. It's not a regulation, which the other three answers are. The other three answers have defined criteria that they must meet to be acceptable.

17. Which of the following environments would make the best use of cross-functional work teams?

    Correct Answer: (D) A project that utilizes all groups across a company
    Explanation: A project that utilizes all groups across a company utilizes cross-functional teams to take advantage of the knowledge and skills available. A data warehouse practice would likely be a Projectized Organization. An offshore company is too vague an answer. Union-approved workplaces is noise.

18. What will the development team have created as a result of completing the work of the project?

    Correct Answer: (C) Project product
    Explanation: The project product is the main output of closing. It is what the project has created. The charter comes from initiation. Work results come from the project execution, which ultimately creates the product of the project. A signed contract is noise.

19. The data warehouse project is reorganized to reflect a projectized structure. Which of the following would be considered an advantage for the team members?

    Correct Answer: (A) Optimization for a single focus on the project
    Explanation: Optimization for a single focus on the project means that the team can focus on what the work of the project is and usually only that. The other answers are associated with Functional Organizations.

20. The project team is in the process of setting expectations with the stakeholders on the project. Which of the following best describes a stakeholder?

    (A) The Project Manager
    (B) A team member
    (C) All the answers
    (D) Someone who works in an area impacted by the work of the project

    Correct Answer: (C) All the answers
    Explanation: The Stakeholder can be anyone impacted by the project. The Stakeholder could be the Sponsor, Senior Management, Project Manager, functional manager, team member, or end user.

21. If the team is in the process of updating a schedule on a project with actuals from the project, which of the following would they use?

    Correct Answer: (B) Control Schedule
    Explanation: The Control Schedule process is the process that is used to control schedule-related items. The Schedule Management Plan is used to establish the rules as they relate to the schedule for the project. The Work Breakdown Structure is the graphical decomposition of the work of the project. The Time Management Plan is noise.

22. A business analyst has a career path that has been very important to her throughout the twelve years of her career. She is put on a project with a projectized structure. Which of the following is likely viewed as a negative of being on the project?

    Correct Answer: (D) Being away from the group and on a project that might make it more difficult to get promoted
    Explanation: Being away from the normal group and not being able to be as easily promoted is the best answer. In a Strong Matrix environment, it will feel fairly similar to a Projectized Organization where skill set specialty in groups will not have as high a priority. The other answers are noise.

23. In a travel agency upgrade project, the Project Manager has been extremely busy. Senior management has begun to become more involved. What is the typical role of Senior Management on a project?

    Correct Answer: (D) Supports the project and resolves resource and other conflict
    Explanation: Senior Management is management that is higher than the Project Manager. They support the project by helping resolve resource issues and other conflicts. The Sponsor pays for the project.

24. The point of sale project is 75% complete at a major retail client. Your company is doing the implementation and has twenty three team members in various locations across five different buildings. Communication and team-building has been a real challenge. Which of the following would fix or improve this problem?

    Correct Answer: (D) Co-location
    Explanation: Co-location is the process of putting personnel closer together or in the same room to help with team-building and project communication. Changing to a functional structure will not gain any benefit, especially this late in the project. Replacing the PM isn't a good option, as that won't fix the issue. Hiring Project Coordinators will add another communication layer to the environment, and this will only complicate communications.

25. Which of the following is considered an advantage of a Functional Organization if you are an accountant?

    Correct Answer: (B) Having a home to go to when the project is complete
    Explanation: Having a home when the project is complete is a key advantage of a Functional Organization. Having more than one boss and more than one project could be characteristics of a Matrix Organization.

26. The project management life cycle is most similar to which of the following?

    Correct Answer: (D) Plan-Do-Check-Act
    Explanation: The Plan-Do-Check-Act is defined by the American Society for Quality as an approach to process development. It can show how the project management life cycle components co-exist or overlap. The project life cycle builds the work of the project. SDLC and use case analysis are software development approaches.

27. The project management team is focusing on the Project Management Life Cycle and the Project Life Cycle. What is the main difference between these two?

    Correct Answer: (D) The Project Management Life Cycle is the Project Management piece of the project and the Project Life Cycle is the process of completing the work of the project.
    Explanation: The Project Management Life Cycle (PMLC) is the Project Management methodology used on a project. The Project Life Cycle applies to whatever is being built. It would be the approach of software for a software project or a building approach for construction.

28. In project management, there are a number of key roles associated with project success. Which role would the Project Manager work with for more funding on the project and involve in the signoff process?

    Correct Answer: (D) The Sponsor
    Explanation: The Sponsor typically pays for the work of the project and owns the work of the project when it is complete.

29. Which of the following is an example of a standard?

    Correct Answer: (D) 700MB capacity for a CD-ROM.
    Explanation: A standard is a measurement for something that is consistent and generally accepted. In this case, the capacity of a CD-ROM is the only "standard" listed in the answers.

30. Which of the following best describes utilizing program management across an organization?

    Correct Answer: (A) Managing of related or similar projects in a coordinated way
    Explanation: Program Management utilizes a coordinated management of related projects. Done for a purpose is a characteristic of a project. The other two answers are noise in this question.

Integration

1. Your point of sale upgrade project is almost complete. You have outsourced the remote installation to three different companies to complete. As the project closes down, what will be done first?

    (A) Close Procurements
    (B) Assignment of contracts for the next phase
    (C) Release of resources
    (D) Closing the project

2. Joe Johnson has signed the charter for the project after evaluating the need for the project. He did this because he will pay for the project, and own what is created when the work is complete. What is his role on this project?

    (A) Senior Management
    (B) Project Management
    (C) Functional Management
    (D) Sponsor

3. The customer has requested a five-week delay on the project while they rebuild a warehouse used for manufacturing a key piece of the project. This delay wasn't planned, but the project couldn't continue without it. The company is limited on available resources. This delay will be best shown in what?

    (A) Network diagram
    (B) Responsibility Assignment Matrix
    (C) Work Breakdown Structure (WBS)
    (D) Budget

4. The company is implementing an enterprise time system across the entire company. This will integrate a number of business units. As a result, it will be very resource-consuming, change a lot of the business processes and could cause reprioritization of other projects that it will replace or modify. Which of the following would concern you most?

    (A) How your raise or promotion might be impacted by not being on the project
    (B) How many resources you can keep
    (C) How many resources you might lose to the new project
    (D) What impact the new project is expected to have on your biggest project

5. As a project functions in a dynamic business and economic environment, which of the following would have the highest priority?

    (A) A change in the company that is creating the project
    (B) A change in the market which the work of the project will operate
    (C) A change in the team on the project
    (D) A change in the project

6. The team has just completed the work on the database project. It has been a long project with significant changes being requested by the customer. Which of the following is the best step to complete next?

    (A) Release of resources
    (B) Lessons Learned
    (C) Formal acceptance
    (D) Procurement audit

7. In establishing project management communication infrastructure, which of the following would be typically used?

    (A) Communication System
    (B) Instant Messaging System
    (C) Information Distribution Planning
    (D) Project Management Information System (PMIS)

8. The Project Manager is meeting with business area owners impacted by his new business process analysis project. He wants to know their project needs plus any constraints and assumptions they might know that would impact his planning attempts positively or negatively. At the same time, the Project Manager is setting project expectations so that their expectations are not out of line with planning. The best description of this is what?

    (A) Change Control Board
    (B) Stakeholder identification
    (C) Team member analysis
    (D) Stakeholder management

9. The project Charter for the grocery store expansion project has just been signed off. There were items in the Charter that described market conditions which could affect the project and also time and cost limitations on the project. These are examples of what?

    (A) Assumptions
    (B) Constraints
    (C) Economic consumption
    (D) Authority level of the Project Manager

10. The team has been having issues with work being done as intended because of scope misinterpretation. They are considering using a Work Authorization System. What is the main purpose of utilizing a Work Authorization System?

    (A) To show who is responsible for what work
    (B) To serve as a time tracking system
    (C) To control Gold Plating
    (D) To show what work is to be done in the project

11. Which of the following best describes a milestone?

    (A) It has a duration of zero (0).
    (B) It is used to define the phase of a project.
    (C) It has a duration of no more than one day.
    (D) It has value in the Charter but not in the plan.

12. When would it make the most sense to close a project?

(A) When a project is cancelled
(B) When a project completes scope verification
(C) All the answers
(D) When a project runs out of money

13. The construction project is in the middle of the executing phase. In evaluating the Triple Constraint which of the following is of the greatest importance?

(A) Time
(B) They are all equal unless otherwise stated in the Charter.
(C) Cost
(D) Quality

14. You are assigned to a new call center project and notice that there are five business units listed as sponsors on the charter. The call center has been discussed at your organization for some time because it has been desperately needed, but this is everyone's first exposure to implementing one. Which of the following would concern you the most about this project?

(A) The Work Breakdown Structure (WBS)
(B) Perform integrated change control
(C) Conflicting goals of the Sponsors
(D) The implementation team

15. The e-commerce project has gone well other than the fact that the Sponsor changed three different times. The project is in closure. All the following would be created in closing except…

(A) Release of resources
(B) Lessons Learned
(C) Project archives
(D) Contract Audit

16. The Project Manager will be starting the executing phase of the construction add-on project next week. The Project Sponsor and Project Manager have a meeting scheduled with the team and the departments that are impacted by the project. They explain what the project is expected to accomplish and how each of the people can help contribute to the success of the project. What is this event called?

(A) Kickoff meeting
(B) Initiation
(C) A verbal Charter
(D) Project management plan development

17. To complete the project scope on time and budget, the Project Manager has worked many hours with a number of conflicts resolved. The team has finally completed project work and is getting customer signoff. When they've achieved this, what will they have accomplished?

(A) Formal Acceptance
(B) Scope verification
(C) Project Archives
(D) Close Procurements

18. All the following would be included in the project management plan except…

    (A) Budget Management Plan
    (B) Schedule Management Plan
    (C) Scope Management Plan
    (D) Risk Management Plan

19. The team has just completed the process of evaluating how the project went. The team members analyzed what worked well and what didn't. They evaluated the planning, executing and change requests. They documented how the Sponsor and Senior Management supported the project. What phase of the project are they in the process of completing?

    (A) Closure
    (B) Controlling
    (C) Executing
    (D) Lessons Learned

20. The Project Manager and team have been working hard to accomplish the milestones of the project work. Because formal acceptance is a goal, what will their efforts be compared to?

    (A) The baseline
    (B) The actuals
    (C) The variance
    (D) The order of magnitude estimate

21. Configuration management involved which of the following as related to project management?

    (A) A thorough Change Control System to ensure the project produces the desired results
    (B) A system used to store versions of software code
    (C) A system used to store versions of documentation on a project
    (D) A piece of an automated Project Management system used to set up project variables

22. You and a team member are having a disagreement about some terminology with Project Management documentation. He asks you where the project management plan is, and when you provide it to him, he says, "I don't need a thesis." You don't understand why he is saying this. Which answer below best describes the confusion?

    (A) He lacks Project Management training.
    (B) He is incorrectly calling a schedule a project management plan.
    (C) You are having a communication breakdown with him.
    (D) You have a really big schedule on the project.

23. The Project Manager and the team have just completed a post project meeting to evaluate successes and failures on the project so they can apply what they learned to future projects. This is known as what?

    (A) Close Procurements
    (B) Lessons Learned
    (C) Closing the project
    (D) Contract Audit

24. The functional manager and Project Manager are arguing about the project management plan and what is needed to create it, as the functional manager is short on resources. Which of the following is the best to create the project management plan?

    (A) Team
    (B) Sponsor
    (C) Project Manager
    (D) Project Manager and team

25. You are the Project Manager on a retail POS System project for Jungle Jim Bookstore. You are fortunate in having the top technical consultant in the company on your project. The corporate headquarters also decides to implement an enterprise reporting system. At the last minute, the CEO pulls your key resource for the new enterprise project. After unsuccessfully lobbying to keep the resource on your project, you concede. What is the best thing to do next?

    (A) Evaluate the impact of the person not being on the project and communicate to Senior Management
    (B) Continue to lobby for the person to be back on your project
    (C) Change the Scope of the project to accommodate for the loss of the resource
    (D) Continue as the original plan, but without the resource

26. The ecommerce project is nearing completion. The team is involved in various activities to close the project. They are grouping together various documents associated with financial records, contracts, internal project documentation, and client-related documentation. What are they in the process of creating?

    (A) Project Closure
    (B) Contract File
    (C) Lessons Learned
    (D) Archives

27. The construction project is about 55% complete and has had its challenges. As of the last status report, it appears to be on track regarding cost, schedule, and scope. You come to understand that the Sponsor has some serious concerns about the project. You don't understand why, based on the last status report. What would be the best thing to do first?

    (A) Ignore Senior Management as the project is in good shape
    (B) Evaluate the schedule and budget to verify the Triple Constraint health of the project
    (C) Meet with the Sponsor and find out what their concerns are
    (D) Tell Senior Management that the project is in good shape

28. You are the Project Manager for a high speed data communications project. You have just finished putting together all the various plans into an integrated document. Which of the following will you do next?

    (A) Perform Integrated Change Control
    (B) Develop Project Management Plan
    (C) Charter Signoff
    (D) Direct and Manage Project Execution

29.   The customer has just attended the weekly meeting for the marketing project and has stated that the market is changing for the product being created. As a result of this change, the customer has requested a significant change to the project. The project is 60% complete. What does the Project Manager do?

   (A) Evaluate the impact to the project and let the customer know the options and impact of the change.
   (B) Make the new work a new project and release the project as is to the market.
   (C) Ignore the customer hoping the change will disappear.
   (D) Tell the customer the project is too close to being complete to integrate the change.

30.   Which of the following would be required to initiate a Change Control System?

   (A) Signoff
   (B) Impact analysis
   (C) Approved changes
   (D) Change Requests

Integration Answer Key

1. Your point of sale upgrade project is almost complete. You have outsourced the remote installation to three different companies to complete. As the project closes down, what will be done first?

   Correct Answer: (A) Close Procurements
   Explanation: Close Procurements occurs before closing the project. Release of resources is part of closing the project. The other answer is noise.

2. Joe Johnson has signed the charter for the project after evaluating the need for the project. He did this because he will pay for the project, and own what is created when the work is complete. What is his role on this project?

   Correct Answer: (D) Sponsor
   Explanation: Typically, the Sponsor's responsibility is to pay for the project and own it when it is complete. Senior Management is responsible for a number of areas on a project. Their main responsibility is to help support the project and resolve resource conflicts as they occur. Remember, unless otherwise stated, for situational questions assume that you are in a Balanced Matrix environment. This will include Functional Managers controlling resources. The Project Manager's responsibility is to drive the completion of the work of the project.

3. The customer has requested a five-week delay on the project while they rebuild a warehouse used for manufacturing a key piece of the project. This delay wasn't planned, but the project couldn't continue without it. The company is limited on available resources. This delay will be best shown in what?

   Correct Answer: (A) Network diagram
   Explanation: The Network diagram shows the sequencing and length of the diagram. The Responsibility Assignment Matrix shows who is responsible for what and doesn't include time. The WBS shows what work is in the project but doesn't focus on how long it should take. The Budget deals with the costs of the project, not time.

4. The company is implementing an enterprise time system across the entire company. This will integrate a number of business units. As a result, it will be very resource-consuming, change a lot of the business processes and could cause reprioritization of other projects that it will replace or modify. Which of the following would concern you most?

   Correct Answer: (D) What impact the new project is expected to have on your biggest project
   Explanation: How the new initiative impacts your biggest project is a valid concern because it could cause your project not to be needed any more. The two options dealing with resources would follow in priority. Your raise or promotion would follow after that.

5. As a project functions in a dynamic business and economic environment, which of the following would have the highest priority?

   Correct Answer: (B) A change in the market which the work of the project will operate
   Explanation: The highest priority in these options would go to the change in the market that could impact the project. This is the case because it would have the biggest impact of all four options. In a bad situation, the market could be radically altered or eliminated. In a good situation, the change could totally reinvent the market, and products that work in that market.

6. The team has just completed the work on the database project. It has been a long project with significant changes being requested by the customer. Which of the following is the best step to complete next?

Correct Answer: (C) Formal acceptance
Explanation: Formal acceptance would be the next step to complete. Verify Scope reveals that the team is done with the work, and that Formal Acceptance is a good next step. Lessons Learned and release of resources are things that would follow the Formal Acceptance. Procurement audit would follow as well if there were an outside party working with the company.

7. In establishing project management communication infrastructure, which of the following would be typically used?

Correct Answer: (D) Project Management Information System (PMIS)
Explanation: The Project Management Information System (PMIS) is a system that is used to store and distribute information on a project. This can be a low tech or high tech system. The other three answers are noise.

8. The Project Manager is meeting with business area owners impacted by his new business process analysis project. He wants to know their project needs plus any constraints and assumptions they might know that would impact his planning attempts positively or negatively. At the same time, the Project Manager is setting project expectations so that their expectations are not out of line with planning. The best description of this is what?

Correct Answer: (D) Stakeholder management
Explanation: Stakeholder management involves determining the needs and expectations of the Stakeholders and management of those needs and expectations. Stakeholder identification involves determining the impacted Stakeholders. The other two answers are noise.

9. The project Charter for the grocery store expansion project has just been signed off. There were items in the Charter that described market conditions which could affect the project and also time and cost limitations on the project. These are examples of what?

Correct Answer: (B) Constraints
Explanation: Constraints are variables that can limit the options the project has. This typically deals with resources, time or money. Assumptions are educated guesses made on the project about items that are not known. The other two answers are noise.

10. The team has been having issues with work being done as intended because of scope misinterpretation. They are considering using a Work Authorization System. What is the main purpose of utilizing a Work Authorization System?

Correct Answer: (C) To control Gold Plating
Explanation: A Work Authorization System helps ensure that certain work is done at a certain time, in a certain order. It helps minimize the opportunity for Gold Plating on a project. The Work Breakdown Structure (WBS) shows what work is to be done on the project. The Responsibility Assignment Matrix (RAM) shows who is responsible for what work. To serve as a time tracking system is noise.

11. Which of the following best describes a milestone?

Correct Answer: (A) It has a duration of zero (0).
Explanation: The milestone has a duration of zero. The milestone is typically used to define the completion of a series of activities. The other three answers are noise in this question.

12.	When would it make the most sense to close a project?

    (A) When a project is cancelled
    (B) When a project completes scope verification
    (C) All the answers
    (D) When a project runs out of money

Correct Answer: (C) All the answers
Explanation: Whenever a project ends it should be formally closed. This allows the team and organization to learn from what worked and didn't on the project, and formally close out the initiative.

13.	The construction project is in the middle of the executing phase. In evaluating the Triple Constraint which of the following is of the greatest importance?

Correct Answer: (B) They are all equal unless otherwise stated in the Charter.
Explanation: The Triple Constraint is Scope, Time, and Cost. Scope is sometimes replaced with Quality. This view is an older view of the Triple Constraint, assuming that quality is associated with what is being built and ignoring the Time and Cost goals. Quality actually looks at the Scope, Time, and Cost parameters of the project. If you see a question like this on the exam, the correct interpretation would be that quality is similar to Scope. The Triple Constraint implies that all three components (Scope, Time, and Cost) are equal unless otherwise defined in the Charter.

14.	You are assigned to a new call center project and notice that there are five business units listed as sponsors on the charter. The call center has been discussed at your organization for some time because it has been desperately needed, but this is everyone's first exposure to implementing one. Which of the following would concern you the most about this project?

Correct Answer: (C) Conflicting goals of the Sponsors
Explanation: Conflicting goals of the Sponsors could significantly impact the project as the attempt to build what would work for all involved could radically alter the plan. The creation of the WBS would be a challenge as well, but not as big as the best answer. The other two answers are noise.

15.	The e-commerce project has gone well other than the fact that the Sponsor changed three different times. The project is in closure. All the following would be created in closing except…

Correct Answer: (D) Contract Audit
Explanation: Contract Audits come from the Contract Closeout process. The other three answers would be expected from Closing the project.

16.	The Project Manager will be starting the executing phase of the construction add-on project next week. The Project Sponsor and Project Manager have a meeting scheduled with the team and the departments that are impacted by the project. They explain what the project is expected to accomplish and how each of the people can help contribute to the success of the project. What is this event called?

Correct Answer: (A) Kickoff meeting
Explanation: The kickoff meeting is what is commonly used on a project to formally start the project. It allows the Sponsor to set expectations, and the team to learn about details of the plan. Initiating produces a Charter. Project management plan development produces a project management plan. A verbal Charter is noise.

17. To complete the project scope on time and budget, the Project Manager has worked many hours with a number of conflicts resolved. The team has finally completed project work and is getting customer signoff. When they've achieved this, what will they have accomplished?

Correct Answer: (A) Formal Acceptance
Explanation: They will have accomplished Formal Acceptance. Scope verification will help lead to this. Close Procurements occurs when closing out a contract with a vendor. Project archives are created when a project is closed out.

18. All the following would be included in the project management plan except…

Correct Answer: (A) Budget Management Plan
Explanation: The Budget Management Plan is noise. The real item associated with cost is called the Cost Management Plan. The other three items are typically in the Project Management Plan.

19. The team has just completed the process of evaluating how the project went. The team members analyzed what worked well and what didn't. They evaluated the planning, executing and change requests. They documented how the Sponsor and Senior Management supported the project. What phase of the project are they in the process of completing?

Correct Answer: (A) Closure
Explanation: They are in the Closing phase. The process described in the question is Lessons Learned. Controlling and executing have already happened on the project.

20. The Project Manager and team have been working hard to accomplish the milestones of the work of the project. As formal acceptance is a goal, what will their efforts be compared to?

Correct Answer: (A) The baseline
Explanation: The baseline is the estimate for the project. It can be for the scope, time, and cost of the project. The Actuals are the real data on what the project has accomplished regarding scope, time, and cost. The variance is the difference between the baseline and actual. The order of magnitude estimate is noise.

21. Configuration management involved which of the following as related to project management?

Correct Answer: (A) A thorough Change Control System to ensure the project produces the desired results
Explanation: Configuration Management involves ensuring that the project is building what it should build. It utilizes a very thorough and detailed change control process to ensure that project results conform to customer needs and requirements.

22. You and a team member are having a disagreement about some terminology with Project Management documentation. He asks you where the project management plan is, and when you provide it to him, he says, "I don't need a thesis." You don't understand why he is saying this. Which answer below best describes the confusion?

Correct Answer: (B) He is incorrectly calling a schedule a project management plan.
Explanation: Many Project Managers incorrectly call a schedule a project management plan. The schedule is actually a part of the project management plan. The project management plan is a cumulative document that contains items such as the schedule, budget, Scope Statement, Work Breakdown Structure, Change Control procedures, and more.

23. The Project Manager and the team have just completed a post project meeting to evaluate successes and failures on the project so they can apply what they learned to future projects. This is known as what?

Correct Answer: (B) Lessons Learned
Explanation: Lessons Learned are valuable tools to learn from success and failure on a project. They can technically happen anywhere on the project, but traditionally happen at the end of a phase or project. The other answers are all part of the project closure process.

24. The functional manager and Project Manager are arguing about the project management plan and what is needed to create it, as the functional manager is short on resources. Which of the following is the best to create the project management plan?

Correct Answer: (D) Project Manager and team
Explanation: The Project Manager and team are the best selection to create the project management plan and the estimates that feed into it. They are the people doing the work, so they should have the opportunity to estimate and plan it as well as possible. The Sponsor pays for the project. The Project Manager or the team only wouldn't be a good choice as both are needed for a realistic plan.

25. You are the Project Manager on a retail POS System project for Jungle Jim Bookstore. You are fortunate in having the top technical consultant in the company on your project. The corporate headquarters also decides to implement an enterprise reporting system. At the last minute, the CEO pulls your key resource for the new enterprise project. After unsuccessfully lobbying to keep the resource on your project, you concede. What is the best thing to do next?

Correct Answer: (A) Evaluate the impact of the person not being on the project and communicate to Senior Management
Explanation: Letting senior management know the impact of not having the resource on the project would be the best thing to do next. You wouldn't change the Scope of the project because that isn't the call of the Project Manager. If you encountered a significant change like the resource leaving, you would be expected to revise the plan to accommodate for the change.

26. The ecommerce project is nearing completion. The team is involved in various activities to close the project. They are grouping together various documents associated with financial records, contracts, internal project documentation, and client-related documentation. What are they in the process of creating?

Correct Answer: (D) Archives
Explanation: Archives are the documents that are created as a result of the project. They can later serve as verification of the details of the project. They happen in closing the project. Lessons Learned happens in closing the project. The contract file is created in the procurement process.

27. The construction project is about 55% complete and has had its challenges. As of the last status report, it appears to be on track regarding cost, schedule, and scope. You come to understand that the Sponsor has some serious concerns about the project. You don't understand why, based on the last status report. What would be the best thing to do first?

Correct Answer: (C) Meet with the Sponsor and find out what their concerns are
Explanation: Meeting with the Sponsor to figure out their concerns is the best solution; it is the most proactive and can provide either an immediate fix or clearest information you can use to identify a concern or problem. The answers involving Senior Management are noise; they don't deal with addressing the problem. The Triple Constraint answer is noise as well.

28. You are the Project Manager for a high speed data communications project. You have just finished putting together all the various plans into an integrated document. Which of the following will you do next?

Correct Answer: (D) Direct and Manage Project Execution

Explanation: After completing the development of the project management plan, the next step listed in the answers is to execute the plan, or do the work of the project. Project management plan development is what the question is describing so that wouldn't be an answer. Perform integrated change control will come as a result of Project management plan execution. The Charter signoff would have been completed before the project planning had started.

29. The customer has just attended the weekly meeting for the marketing project and has stated that the market is changing for the product being created. As a result of this change, the customer has requested a significant change to the project. The project is 60% complete. What does the Project Manager do?

Correct Answer: (A) Evaluate the impact to the project and let the customer know the options and impact of the change.

Explanation: The Project Manager needs to evaluate the impact to the project and let the customer know the options. The Project Manager is there to do what the customer needs according to the plan or modified plan. Telling the customer the project is too close to being complete to integrate the change wouldn't be the Project Manager's decision to make, neither would defining the work as a new project. Ignoring the customer and hoping things disappear is professionally irresponsible.

30. Which of the following would be required to initiate a Change Control System?

Correct Answer: (D) Change Requests

Explanation: Change Requests involve a desired change that hasn't been approved yet. Approved changes are the output of a Change Control System. These are Change Requests that have gone into the system and been approved. Impact analysis involves identifying what impact the change might have on the project or environment. Signoff involves receiving approval. In this case, signoff is noise.

Scope

1. For the last month, the team has attempted to obtain sign off from the customer on the Internet project. The main deliverable and results of the test plan were sent to the customer, but so far after one month, the customer has not acknowledged receiving it. Which of the following is the best action to take?

    (A) Communicate to Senior Management for assistance
    (B) Ask the customer's supervisor why they haven't acknowledged it
    (C) Document the issue in the issue log
    (D) Stop work on the project until the customer acknowledges and approves the deliverable

2. A new toll way and bridge project is being planned to go over Lake Wabaunsee. This project involves creating six new lanes within the existing road and adding three toll booths along with the bridge. Because of where the new project is being built, it is impossible to shut down lanes of traffic during the weekdays. The lanes can be shut down only during the evenings after midnight or on weekends. This is an example of what?

    (A) Successful buyer negotiations
    (B) Constraints
    (C) Assumptions
    (D) Negotiation points

3. Which of the following best describes a milestone used on a project?

    (A) It has a duration of no more than one day.
    (B) It has value in the Charter but not in the plan.
    (C) It has a duration of zero (0).
    (D) It is used to define the phase of a project.

4. In creating a Work Breakdown Structure (WBS) on the project, the team would consider all the following applicable except...

    (A) The team and the Project Manager should be involved in creating it.
    (B) It will resemble an organizational chart in appearance when complete.
    (C) The activity sequencing of the WBS can be done only in parallel.
    (D) It is a Decomposition of the work of the project.

5. Project A is four months long, has four Stakeholders, and has completed planning. Project B is 12 months long, has 10 Stakeholders, and is in execution. Project C is 12 months long, has four Stakeholders, and is in planning. Which project is most likely to experience Scope creep?

    (A) Project A
    (B) Project B
    (C) Project C
    (D) Not enough Information

6. A new call center is being built to support a new product at a satellite Internet company. The company doesn't have any data associated with the time frames needed to complete a customer order. This data is important because it will help determine the number of employees needed in the call center. The company performs some tests to try to determine how long it will take to complete a customer order. This test data is then incorporated into the projections and planning. What has the company just created?

    (A) Staff acquisition
    (B) Constraints
    (C) Assumptions
    (D) Team development

7. The Project Manager is utilizing a new set of planning tools that are a great deal more detailed than he has used before. One tool he uses is a WBS dictionary. What can a WBS dictionary do for the project?

    (A) Control Gold Plating
    (B) Provide task definitions
    (C) Verify the Scope of the project
    (D) Define the work of the project

8. A new manufacturing facility is being built for a consumer electronic company. The project to create it is nearing completion and will soon begin to enter the closing phase. This will involve a number of people, but who will ultimately approve the work of the project?

    (A) The customer
    (B) Stakeholders
    (C) Senior Management
    (D) Project Manager

9. The project team has just started breaking down the components of the Web development project into smaller pieces that are can easier manage. After doing this, what level of decomposition will they ultimately stop at?

    (A) Verifying scope
    (B) Defining scope
    (C) Defining activities
    (D) Creating the WBS

10. The project team is involved in created the Work Breakdown Structure of the project. Which of the following best describes a Work Breakdown Structure (WBS) that will be created?

    (A) If the work is not listed in the WBS, it is not in the project.
    (B) All the answers
    (C) The accumulation of the work in the WBS should be equal to the work of the project.
    (D) The work should be decomposed to a realistic level of detail.

11. Which of the following makes the most sense for creating a Work Breakdown Structure?

    (A) It provides authority for the Project Manager.
    (B) It allows the project budget to be determined.
    (C) It helps attain buy-in from the team doing the work.
    (D) It allows the project completion date to be determined.

12. The project team and their manager have been working hard to prepare the estimate for the new warehouse project. They have defined the scope of the project and are now working on the Work Breakdown Structure. The Work Breakdown Structure represents what on a project?

    (A) The schedule
    (B) The Decomposition of the task list
    (C) The Decomposition of the work of the project
    (D) The task list of the project

13. The trade show project team has just begun breaking down the pieces of the project into smaller easier to maintain and manage pieces. This is known as what?

    (A) Define Scope
    (B) Verify Scope
    (C) Creating the WBS
    (D) Collect Requirements

14. The Project Manager and team are involved in project planning on a new technology project at their company which will utilize an untested technology associated with biorhythms. They are in the process of breaking the work down into the smaller more manageable pieces ultimately leading to activities. What are they creating?

    (A) Work package
    (B) Activity definition
    (C) To-do list
    (D) Task list

15. The charter is signed on the project and planning can begin. Senior Management wants you to begin planning as soon as possible. If you are in the process of planning the project, what is the best way to schedule scope verification?

    (A) At the end of every phase on the project
    (B) After the Sponsor defines what they want the project to create
    (C) When the project management plan is awaiting signoff
    (D) When the work of the project is done

16. If the Project Manager is concerned about satisfying a customer, which of the following will they pay the most attention to?

    (A) Work Breakdown Structure (WBS)
    (B) Scope verification
    (C) A signed contract
    (D) Gold Plating

17. The Project Manager and her team have been working with the Sponsor over the last three weeks to determine what work is needed in the project and any work that is not as well. This is known as what?

    (A) Control Scope
    (B) Verify Scope
    (C) Define Scope
    (D) Collect Requirements

18. Which of the following represents a rule of thumb associated with the WBS decomposition process?

    (A) Creating a WBS where the summary tasks are equal to the detail underneath it
    (B) Breaking work down to realistic level where work packages are the lowest level
    (C) Breakdown the work of the project until it is done by a single resource
    (D) Using an organizational structure appearance

19. The Project Manager is working with the customer to gain formal acceptance on the project deliverables. The customer is saying that five of the deliverables are not aligned with project goals, and are unusable in their present form. Which of the following will be used to correct the problem?

    (A) Scope analysis
    (B) Team-building
    (C) Control Scope
    (D) Verify Scope

20. John is new to project management. There are a number of new things he is trying to use to do his new job well. He has learned about how breaking things down to smaller pieces can help improve project success. All the following are breakdown structures he might consider using in project management except…

    (A) Risk breakdown structure
    (B) Resource breakdown structure
    (C) Bill of materials
    (D) Communication breakdown structure

21. The team is in the process of completing the Work Breakdown Structure of the project. Once they have completed this, which of the following can they begin to work on?

    (A) Estimate Costs
    (B) Develop Schedule
    (C) Estimate Activity Durations
    (D) All the answers

22. The Project Manager is in the process of defining the Scope for the project that will last over three years. As she proceeds with this step, which of the items below will she be most concerned about?

    (A) The list of preferred vendors for outsourcing
    (B) The Work Breakdown Structure (WBS)
    (C) Create it as quickly as possible to continue planning
    (D) Verify that all key Stakeholders have provided their input

23. The team is involved in determining what the scope management plan for the project will be. Which of the following will they need to start this?

    (A) Project Charter
    (B) Work Breakdown Structure
    (C) Control Scope System
    (D) Change Requests

24.   The team is involved in breaking the work of the project into smaller pieces. Which answer below best describes when this will happen?

(A) Creating the WBS and Define Activity
(B) Control Costs
(C) Control Schedule
(D) Collect Requirements and Control Scope

25.   The Project Manager is working with the customer to establish an interpretation of what the customer needs the new project to create. They discuss what the project will and will not include. When they are done, the interpretation will be used to decompose the work further, ultimately ending up in the schedule. What is the Project Manager creating?

(A) Work breakdown structure
(B) Verify Scope
(C) Scope change request
(D) Scope statement

26.   The project to upgrade the customer care system is approximately 75% complete when a senior manager says that a major change needs to occur with the scope of the project or the system will be useless when it's rolled out. He further explains this would delay the anticipated finish date of the project. After he explains the details of the proposed change in Scope, what do you do first?

(A) Implement a change control to incorporate the new work
(B) Let him know what the delay to the project would be
(C) Meet with the team to determine the impact
(D) Tell him no, because it will change the finish date of the project

27.   The Project Manager is working with the sponsor to attain formal acceptance on the infrastructure project deliverables. The customer says that seven of the deliverables are not meeting project goals and are unusable in their present form. Upon reviewing documentation, the sponsor explains to the Project Manager that the requirements are not accurate to meet the needs for which the project was planned. What part of the planning process did this problem occur?

(A) Control Scope
(B) Creating the work breakdown structure
(C) Verify Scope
(D) Define Scope

28. The electronic monitoring equipment project has entered closure. As the Project Manager and the team prepare for closure, they are told that scope verification will be key to the success of the project. Why is this?

    (A) Scope verification is the process of comparing what the project created to the Scope Statement, product description, and anything else that helps ensure the results of the project will function as intended.
    (B) Scope verification is used to verify that the project team understands the Scope of the project.
    (C) Scope verification should have been done earlier in the project and since it wasn't done then, it's important to complete it before the project is complete.
    (D) Scope verification validates that the Sponsor signed the Scope Statement at the beginning of planning.

29. The medical software project has been going on for two years with a large number of changes and issues. The Project Manager is getting ready for the project to be completed. Which of the following will help close the project?

    (A) Team development
    (B) Scope verification
    (C) Planning for the next project
    (D) Release of resources

30. Which of the following is the most accurate statement about a milestone?

    (A) It has slack of zero
    (B) It is only used in the scope statement
    (C) It can represent the beginning or completion of a deliverable, work package, phase or project
    (D) It is only used with the charter

Scope Answer Key

1. For the last month, the team has attempted to get sign off from the customer on the Internet project. The main deliverable and results of the test plan were sent to the customer, but so far after one month, the customer has not acknowledged receiving it. Which of the following is the best action to take?

    Correct Answer: (A) Communicate to Senior Management for assistance
    Explanation: If the customer is not fulfilling his expectations of the project and the Project Manager has communicated to the customer already, then Senior Management would be the role that would provide assistance. Stopping work and asking the customer's supervisor would be unprofessional. Documenting the issue and doing nothing else would be inappropriate because a Project Manager should be proactive in addressing problems.

2. A new toll way and bridge project is being planned to go over Lake Wabaunsee. This project involves creating six new lanes within the existing road and adding three toll booths along with the bridge. Because of where the new project is being built, it is impossible to shut down lanes of traffic during the weekdays. The lanes can be shut down only during the evenings after midnight or on weekends. This is an example of what?

    Correct Answer: (B) Constraints
    Explanation: Constraints are pieces of the project that limit the options available on the project. Negotiation points could fit here, but is not the best answer. Assumptions come into play when we don't know something on a project. Successful buyer negotiation is noise.

3. Which of the following best describes a milestone used on a project?

    Correct Answer: (C) It has a duration of zero (0).
    Explanation: The milestone has a duration of zero. The milestone is typically used to define the completion of a series of activities. The other three answers are noise in this question.

4. In creating a Work Breakdown Structure (WBS) on the project, the team would consider all the following applicable except...

    Correct Answer: (C) The activity sequencing of the WBS can be done only in parallel.
    Explanation: The activity sequencing of the WBS can be done only in parallel is a noise answer because it makes no logical sense. The other three answers are characteristic of a Work Breakdown Structure (WBS).

5. Project A is four months long, has four Stakeholders, and has completed planning. Project B is 12 months long, has 10 Stakeholders, and is in execution. Project C is 12 months long, has four Stakeholders, and is in planning. Which project is most likely to experience Scope creep?

    Correct Answer: (B) Project B
    Explanation: Project B is tied for the longest project but has the most Stakeholders. The longer the project and greater the number of Stakeholders involved, the more an environment is prone to Scope creep.

6.   A new call center is being built to support a new product at a satellite Internet company. The company doesn't have any data associated with the time frames needed to complete a customer order. This data is important because it will help determine the number of employees needed in the call center. The company performs some tests to try to determine how long it will take to complete a customer order. This test data is then incorporated into the projections and planning. What has the company just created?

Correct Answer: (C) Assumptions

Explanation: Assumptions are created when there is an absence of certain information on a project. It's an educated guess. As the project evolves, the assumptions should be fewer. Constraints are items that limit a project environment. Team Development and Staff Acquisition are noise.

7.   The Project Manager is utilizing a new set of planning tools that are a great deal more detailed than he has used before. One tool he uses is a WBS dictionary. What can a WBS dictionary do for the project?

Correct Answer: (A) Control Gold Plating

Explanation: The WBS dictionary focuses on defining what work should happen in what order. Thus, it helps create a structure for only the work of the project to be done in the right sequence and can help eliminate Gold Plating. Defining the work of the project would be done before the WBS dictionary. Verifying the Scope of the project would be done after the work of the project is complete. Providing task definitions is noise.

8   A new manufacturing facility is being built for a consumer electronic company. The project to create it is nearing completion and will soon begin to enter the closing phase. This will involve a number of people, but who will ultimately approve the work of the project?

Correct Answer: (A) The customer

Explanation: The customer ultimately approves (or verifies) the Scope of the project. The Project Manager will likely perform an initial verification before showing the customer, but the customer has the ultimate signoff. The Stakeholder is too vague of an answer. Senior Management is not as good an answer as the customer.

9.   The project team has just started breaking down the components of the Web development project into smaller pieces that are can easier manage. After doing this what level of decomposition will they ultimately stop at?

Correct Answer: (C) Defining Activities

Explanation: Creating the WBS involves taking the Scope of the project and breaking it down into smaller pieces that are easier to define, estimate, and manage. Verifying scope compares the scope of the project to work results. After that, the team continues to decompose the project work packages, stopping at defining activities when they have created activity lists.

10. The project team is involved in created the Work Breakdown Structure of the project. Which of the following best describes a Work Breakdown Structure (WBS) that will be created?

(A) If the work is not listed in the WBS, it is not in the project.
(B) All the answers
(C) The accumulation of the work in the WBS should be equal to the work of the project.
(D) The work should be decomposed to a realistic level of detail.

Correct Answer: (B) All the answers

Explanation: A WBS includes all the work in the project. If it is not listed in the WBS, it's not part of the project. A WBS should be decomposed to a realistic level of detail. Not breaking it down far enough can have work slipping through the cracks and breaking it down into too much detail can turn the project into micro-management. Adding up the work in the WBS should equal the work that is in the project.

11. Which of the following makes the most sense for creating a Work Breakdown Structure?

     Correct Answer: (C) It helps attain buy-in from the team doing the work.
     Explanation: The WBS has a number of positives. The best one of the options in the question is to help get buy-in from the people doing the work. If they aren't involved in the creation of the plan, it's not as easy to get the buy-in and the planning likely won't be as accurate as it could be when the people doing the work are involved. The WBS focuses on the WHAT of the project, so the completion date wouldn't come from the WBS. Authority comes from the Charter. Estimate Costs and budgeting deals with the project budget.

12. The project team and their manager have been working hard to prepare the estimate for the new warehouse project. They have defined the scope of the project and are now working on the Work Breakdown Structure. The Work Breakdown Structure represents what on a project?

     Correct Answer: (C) The Decomposition of the work of the project
     Explanation: The WBS represents the Decomposition of the work of the project. If the work is shown in the WBS, it is in the project; if it's not shown there, it's not in the project. The task list is created during Define Activity process, and the schedule is created after the WBS.

13. The trade show project team has just begun breaking down the pieces of the project into smaller easier to maintain and manage pieces. This is known as what?

     Correct Answer: (C) Creating the WBS
     Explanation: Creating the WBS process involves taking the Scope of the project and breaking it down into smaller pieces that are easier to define, estimate, and manage. Verify Scope is comparing the Scope of the project to work results. Collect Requirements involves determining the Scope Statement and Scope management approach for the project. Define Scope involves establishing the Scope Statement of the project.

14. The Project Manager and team are involved in project planning on a new technology project at their company which will utilize an untested technology associated with biorhythms. They are in the process of breaking the work down into the smaller more manageable pieces ultimately leading to activities. What are they creating?

     Correct Answer: (A) Work package
     Explanation: The work package is the smallest level that the WBS is broken into. The next level of Decomposition is to create activity definitions, which are sometimes known as task lists. A to-do list is noise in this question.

15. The charter is signed on the project and planning can begin. Senior Management wants you to begin planning as soon as possible. If you are in the process of planning the project, what is the best way to schedule scope verification?

     Correct Answer: (A) At the end of every phase on the project
     Explanation: It is better to verify scope more frequently on a project instead of simply waiting until the end. This allows adjustment of work as the project evolves in case something is determined incorrect or insufficient earlier in the project. Scheduling it after the sponsors define what they want the project to create would be too early in the project to verify scope.

16. If the Project Manager is concerned about satisfying a customer, which of the following will they pay the most attention to?

    Correct Answer: (B) Scope verification
    Explanation: Scope verification means that the work of the project has been verified to meet the needs of the project. If this is successful, it should provide customer satisfaction. A WBS is simply part of the planning process. Gold Plating is providing the customers something they didn't ask for. A signed contract is noise.

17. The Project Manager and her team have been working with the Sponsor over the last three weeks to determine what work is needed in the project and any work that is not as well. This is known as what?

    Correct Answer: (C) Define Scope
    Explanation: Define Scope involves determining the Scope Statement for the project. The Scope Statement generally defines what is and is not in the project. Collect Requirements involves determining the scope management approach for the project. Verify Scope compares the Scope of the project to work results. Control Scope comes into the process after the plan has been signed off and is in Project Plan Execution.

18. Which of the following represents a rule of thumb associated with the WBS decomposition process?

    Correct Answer: (B) Breaking work down to realistic level where work packages are the lowest level
    Explanation: A general rule of thumb is to break the work of the project work packages. Breaking work packages or tasks down to a single resource assigned is not always practical. Creating a WBS where the summary tasks are equal to the detail underneath it is a characteristic of a WBS. Using an organizational structure appearance is noise.

19. The Project Manager is working with the customer to gain formal acceptance on the project deliverables. The customer is saying that five of the deliverables are not aligned with project goals, and are unusable in their present form. Which of the following will be used to correct the problem?

    Correct Answer: (C) Control Scope
    Explanation: Control Scope is used to review and approve or reject scope change requests to the project. Scope analysis is noise. Team-building would be used to help the group of people on the project become more productive. That is not applicable to this situation. Verify Scope helps validate that the project created what it was to create. That is the process that discovered the problem of the difference in scope planned and created.

20. John is new to project management. There are a number of new things he is trying to use to do his new job well. He has learned about how breaking things down to smaller pieces can help improve project success. All the following are breakdown structures he might consider using in project management except...

    Correct Answer: (D) Communication breakdown structure
    Explanation: The communication breakdown structure is a noise answer. It doesn't exist. The bill of materials is used to show all the pieces of an assembly. The Risk Breakdown Structure is used to decompose the risks on a project. The Resource Breakdown Structure is used to show resource being utilized on a project, regardless of their association with any functional organization.

21. The team is in the process of completing the Work Breakdown Structure of the project. Once they have completed this, which of the following can they begin to work on?

    (A) Estimate Costs
    (B) Develop Schedule
    (C) Estimate Activity Durations
    (D) All the answers

    Correct Answer: (D) All the answers
    Explanation: The WBS serves as a primary input for determining what types of resources, and their durations are needed on the project, what the high level costs should be for the project, and what shape the schedule will take when complete.

22. The Project Manager is in the process of defining the Scope for the project that will last over three years. As she proceeds with this step, which of the items below will she be most concerned about?

    Correct Answer: (D) Verify that all key Stakeholders have provided their input
    Explanation: Verifying that all key Stakeholders have provided their input is the most important item. If this doesn't happen, the project could be delayed or derailed. The WBS isn't addressed in Collect Requirements. The other two answers are noise.

23. The team is involved in determining what the scope management plan for the project will be. Which of the following will they need to start this?

    Correct Answer: (A) Project Charter
    Explanation: The Project Charter is an input into Collect Requirements, because it provides the foundation of the project and allows the Collect Requirements to begin. The WBS is an output of Define Scope. Change-related items don't show up in the process yet. Collect Requirements is still in the planning process.

24. The team is involved in breaking the work of the project into smaller pieces. Which answer below best describes when this will happen?

    Correct Answer: (A) Creating the WBS and Define Activity
    Explanation: The work of the project is decomposed in creating the WBS to establish work packages and Define Activity to create task lists. Control Schedule and Control Costs deal with maintaining control of the Schedule and Cost, not Decomposition. Collect Requirements and Control Scope are noise.

25. The Project Manager is working with the customer to establish an interpretation of what the customer needs the new project to create. They discuss what the project will and will not include. When they are done, the interpretation will be used to decompose the work further, ultimately ending up in the schedule. What is the Project Manager creating?

    Correct Answer: (D) Scope statement
    Explanation: The Scope Statement defines what is and is not in the scope of the project. The Work Breakdown Structure shows only what work is in the project. A Scope Change Request involves modifying the scope of the project to reflect different work. Verify Scope involves validation of what was created being in alignment with the defined scope of the project.

26. The project to upgrade the customer care system is approximately 75% complete when a senior manager says that a major change needs to occur with the scope of the project or the system will be useless when it's rolled out. He further explains this would delay the anticipated finish date of the project. After he explains the details of the proposed change in Scope, what do you do first?

Correct Answer: (C) Meet with the team to determine the impact
Explanation: Meet with the team to determine the impact before letting Senior Management and the Sponsor know of the impacts. This will allow them to make the proper decision, if this indeed would violate the finish date defined in the Charter. It's key in the situational questions not to tell a senior manager or Sponsor "no," but instead let them know the options and impact associated with the request. You cannot explain the delay to the project until the team helps determine what the project impacts are. A change control of this size would likely not be implemented by a Project Manager, but more likely by the Senior Management or Sponsor.

27. The Project Manager is working with the sponsor to attain formal acceptance on the infrastructure project deliverables. The customer says that seven of the deliverables are not meeting project goals and are unusable in their present form. Upon reviewing documentation, the sponsor explains to the Project Manager that the requirements are not accurate to meet the needs for which the project was planned. What part of the planning process did this problem occur?

Correct Answer: (D) Define Scope
Explanation: Define Scope is used to create the Scope Statement of the project. Verify Scope involves attaining Formal Acceptance of the work of the project. Creating the WBS involves the decomposition of the project resulting in work packages at the lowest level of decomposition. Control Scope is used to review and approve or reject scope change requests to the project.

28. The electronic monitoring equipment project has entered closure. As the Project Manager and the team prepare for closure, they are told that scope verification will be key to the success of the project. Why is this?

Correct Answer: (A) Scope verification is the process of comparing what the project created to the Scope Statement, product description, and anything else that helps ensure the results of the project will function as intended.
Explanation: Scope verification is used to compare work results of the project created to what was planned to be built. This can include using the Scope Statement, Work Breakdown Structure (WBS), or product description. If the verification process is satisfactory then the work of the project is typically viewed acceptable.

29. The medical software project has been going on for two years with a large number of changes and issues. The Project Manager is getting ready for the project to be completed. Which of the following will help close the project?

Correct Answer: (B) Scope verification
Explanation: Scope verification involves validating that the project created what was described to be created. Team development is a process that goes on throughout the project. Planning for the next project is not appropriate while the project is still ongoing. Release of resources will happen around this point in the project, but it will not help close the project.

30. Which of the following is the most accurate statement about a milestone?

Correct Answer: (C) It can represent the beginning or completion of a deliverable, work package, phase or project
Explanation: A milestone can be used to represent the beginning or completion of something significant on the project. This could also include a phase or project. A milestone would have slack of only zero if it were on the critical path of the schedule. Milestones are used throughout the Project Management Plan, not just in the Scope Statement or the Charter.

Time

1. Crosswind Custom Homes is building a customer's dream house. However, the general contractor has to attend to another development. This causes a three week delay because she has no backup and is required to be there for the signoff of the plans. This event causes a delay in the completion of the house. This is an example of what?

    (A) External Dependencies
    (B) Crashing
    (C) Mandatory Dependencies
    (D) Lag

2. The software team is building a new application for their company. This is a new product type at their company, and the market for the product is extremely unstable and volatile. According to the product manager, a key to success will be flexibility to adapt the product to the market changes that will occur during software development. Which scheduling type best fits this need?

    (A) Crashing
    (B) Rolling wave planning
    (C) Precedence diagramming
    (D) Fast Tracking

3. Which of the following predecessors would a Project Manager use for an Activity on Arrow (AOA) diagram?

    (A) Start to Start (SS)
    (B) Finish to Start (FS)
    (C) Start to Finish (SF)
    (D) Finish to Finish (FF)

4. Which of the following best represents a lag that would be used on an Activity on Node diagram.

    (A) The Critical Path
    (B) The earliest a new system can be ordered from the manufacturer
    (C) A delay after the sheetrock (wall board) is done in a house to allow it to dry before continuing work in that area
    (D) The latest a new system can be ordered from the manufacturer without delaying the project

5. Calculate the variance for the following: Pessimistic=14, Optimistic=6, Realistic=8.

    (A) 1.78
    (B) 1.33
    (C) Not enough information
    (D) 8.66

6. The road construction project is twelve weeks behind schedule with ten team members working on it. Five of these team members are working on the Critical Path related items. What is the Slack of the Critical Path?

(A) Negative twelve weeks
(B) 30
(C) 0 (Zero)
(D) Not enough information

7. Crosswind Custom Construction is building a shopping center. However, rain has delayed the finish by two weeks. The Project Manager is evaluating various ways to compress the schedule. The Project Manager suspects that the windows and climate control could occur at the same time instead of right after each other as laid out in the schedule. It is then discovered that local zoning laws will not allow this. This is an example of what?

(A) Crashing
(B) Mandatory Dependencies
(C) Discretionary Dependencies
(D) External Dependencies

8. You and a fellow Project Manager are having a discussion about his project. He says the Network diagram for it has four paths that have the maximum duration of 25 units on the diagram. He says he doesn't have a Critical Path because they are all the same length, and you can only have one Critical Path. Which of the following is a true statement?

(A) The Critical Path is the shortest path on the project.
(B) You can have more than one Critical Path, but they are the longest paths on the project, and more than one Critical Path will increase your project risk.
(C) You can have more than one Critical Path, but they are the shortest paths not the longest.
(D) You can have more than one Critical Path, but they are the longest paths on the project, and more than one Critical Path will decrease your project risk.

9. The Project Manager is creating an estimate for building a cellular infrastructure base station. It is something that is new to the Project Manager and his team. They decide to create a bottom-up estimate. All the following are advantages of this type of estimate except…

(A) It provides supporting detail of the estimate.
(B) It provides team buy in when they help create it.
(C) It takes a great amount of time to create.
(D) There is a greater degree of accuracy because of the detail it was created at.

10. The project team is working together on creating the plan for the data cleansing project. They have had some challenges associated with the planning. They are in the process of creating a Network diagram. What will this show the team?

(A) The schedule
(B) The duration estimate of the project
(C) The sequencing of the tasks on the project
(D) The Decomposition of the work of the project

11. The Project Manager is creating an estimate for building a warehouse and distribution center. It is a project similar to what he builds about 3 times a year. He is using the rule of thumb of $100 per square foot to calculate the estimate. What type of estimate is this?

    (A) Parametric
    (B) Analogous
    (C) Gut feel
    (D) Bottom up

12. The road construction project is going well. There is a scope change adding four new exits and two additional lanes, as a result, a new team is brought in to assist the existing team in the new scope of the project. Upon arriving, the team asks to see where the project currently stands. What are they asking for?

    (A) Milestone chart
    (B) Gantt chart
    (C) Work Breakdown Structure
    (D) Network diagram

13. The construction team is behind schedule on its project. The customer is considering giving the project to another company if they cannot get the project back on track. The team is considering putting more resources on the critical path to accelerate the schedule. This is an example of what?

    (A) Staff Acquisition
    (B) Crashing
    (C) Re-planning
    (D) Fast Tracking

14. The construction team is behind schedule on their project. The customer is considering giving the project to another company to complete if they cannot get the project back on track. The team is considering re-sequencing the Critical Path areas on the Network diagram to shorten the length of the schedule. This is an example of what?

    (A) Crashing
    (B) Staff Acquisition
    (C) Fast Tracking
    (D) Re-planning

15. Calculate the standard deviation for the following: Pessimistic=14, Optimistic=6, Realistic=8.

    (A) 1.33
    (B) 1.78
    (C) 8.66
    (D) Not enough information

16. You are putting together the final schedule on your security encryption project. The problem you are having is that you don't have a consistent usage of your resources. Some are working 2 hours a day, some 16 hours a day, and there are some days when they aren't scheduled to work at all. Which of the following below would fix this problem?

   (A) Resource Leveling
   (B) PERT Analysis
   (C) Fast Tracking
   (D) Crashing

17. Which of the following utilizes a dummy?

   (A) Activity on Arrow (AOA)
   (B) GERT
   (C) Activity on Node (AON)
   (D) Gantt chart

18. Which of the following would the team member use to determine the float on a project?

   (A) Late Start-Early Start (LS-ES)
   (B) Late Finish-Early Finish (LF-EF)
   (C) A and B
   (D) Late Finish-Late Start (LF-LS)

19. Crosswind Custom Websites is building an ecommerce system. However, conflicting priorities from other projects has delayed the finish by two weeks. The schedule shows that the next task is to define the requirements needed by the customer, then that is followed by the coding. This is an example of what?

   (A) Lag
   (B) Crashing
   (C) Discretionary Dependencies
   (D) Mandatory Dependencies

20. The Project Manager is creating an estimate for a housing development. This is something for which he is quite experienced. The client needs the estimate in four hours. Which of the following types of estimates make the most sense to use?

   (A) Gut Feel
   (B) Parametric
   (C) Bottom up
   (D) Analogous

21. You are the Project Manager on a merger and acquisition project. Task A (3 days) and Task B (4 days) can start immediately. Task C (2 days) can start after A and B are complete. Task D (5 days) can begin after task B is complete. Task E (6 days) can begin after task B is complete. Task F (4 days) can begin after tasks C and D are complete. Task G (5 days) can begin after tasks D and E are complete. Task H (4 days) can begin after tasks G and H are complete. What is the Critical Path?

    (A) BDFH
    (B) ACFH
    (C) BEGH
    (D) BCFH

22. In the original Network diagram question, if Task D increases from five to eight days, what is the Critical Path, and what is the length?

    (A) BCFH, 18 days
    (B) BDGH, 21 days
    (C) BDFH, 20 days
    (D) ACFH, 16 days

23. Using the original Network diagram question, what is the Slack of Task D?

    (A) Two days
    (B) One day
    (C) Four days
    (D) Not enough information

24. The construction team is building a new design for their company. This is a new design type at their company, and the market for the product is extremely unstable because of current interest rates. According to the site manager, a key to success will be to have an extremely accurate estimate on the resource needs for the project, because the company is resource constrained. Which type of duration estimating approach is the most accurate?

    (A) Parametric estimating
    (B) Bottom-up estimating
    (C) Analogous estimating
    (D) Fast tracking

25. The auto manufacturing plant upgrade project is underway after some initial delays associated with the labor union approving the work. The labor union removes the workers from the project one day because the labor contract has been violated. They discover this was from a vendor requiring union personnel to do work that was not covered in the contract. Without this work being complete as needed, the project cannot continue. This is an example of what?

    (A) Discretionary dependency
    (B) A city employee not wanting to do his job
    (C) Mandatory dependency
    (D) External dependency

26. Which of the following is the most accurate definition of a lag?

    (A) The amount of time a task can be delayed without delaying the project finish date
    (B) A delay inserted between tasks
    (C) Slack
    (D) Float

27. Crosswind Custom Websites is building a huge ecommerce system. However, the designer getting sick has delayed the finish by two weeks. The Project Manager evaluates the schedule and determines that the graphics and backend work could occur at the same time instead of right after each other, as laid out in the schedule. This is an example of what?

    (A) Crashing
    (B) Fast tracking
    (C) Lag
    (D) Mandatory Dependencies

28. Calculate the PERT estimate for the following: Pessimistic= 14, Optimistic= 6, Realistic= 8.

    (A) 1.78
    (B) 1.33
    (C) Not enough information
    (D) 8.66

29. The housing development project is progressing well. The bank vice president who is the executive Sponsor gets promoted and moves to a new branch. His replacement is brought in from a new area and, upon arrival, asks to see where the project currently stands. Which of the following do you show him?

    (A) Work Breakdown Structure
    (B) Network diagram
    (C) Milestone chart
    (D) Gantt chart

30. Float on a Network diagram is also known as:

    (A) PERT
    (B) Lag
    (C) GERT
    (D) Slack

Time Answer Key

1. Crosswind Custom Homes is building a customer's dream house. However, the general contractor has to attend to another development. This causes a three week delay because she has no backup and is required to be there for the signoff of the plans. This event causes a delay in the completion of the house. This is an example of what?

   Correct Answer: (A) External Dependencies
   Explanation: The external dependency is a dependency that is out of the control of the internal organization. In this case the company building the house is dependent on the availability of the general contractor. Since that person is unavailable for signoff for three weeks, it is an external dependency. Mandatory is required but internal to the organization. Crashing and Lag are noise in this question.

2. The software team is building a new application for their company. This is a new product type at their company, and the market for the product is extremely unstable and volatile. According to the product manager, a key to success will be flexibility to adapt the product to the market changes that will occur during software development. Which scheduling type best fits this need?

   Correct Answer: (B) Rolling wave planning
   Explanation: In an environment where there is a great degree of flexibility or instability it's good to use a rolling wave planning approach. This allows the team to plan out as much as reasonably possible, and as they are executing that part of the plan, they continue to plan future work as they learn more about it. Crashing involves putting more resources on the critical path tasks. Fast tracking involves re-sequencing already defined tasks to compress the overall duration of the schedule. Precedence diagramming is a network diagramming technique.

3. Which of the following predecessors would a Project Manager use for an Activity on Arrow (AOA) diagram?

   Correct Answer: (B) Finish to Start (FS)
   Explanation: Activity on Arrow (AOA) diagramming uses the (FS) Finish to Start predecessor. The other three answers work ONLY within the AON (Activity on Node) or PDM (Precedence Diagramming Method).

4. Which of the following best represents a lag that would be used on an Activity on Node diagram?

   Correct Answer: (C) A delay after the sheetrock (wall board) is done in a house to allow it to dry before continuing work in that area
   Explanation: A delay after the sheetrock is done to allow it to dry before continuing work in that area is an example of a Lag.

5. Calculate the variance for the following: Pessimistic=14, Optimistic=6, Realistic=8.

   Correct Answer: (A) 1.78
   Explanation: The formula for variance is Pessimistic-Optimistic divided by 6, squared. The answer is 1.78.

6. The road construction project is twelve weeks behind schedule with ten team members working on it. Five of these team members are working on the Critical Path related items. What is the Slack of the Critical Path?

    Correct Answer: (A) Negative twelve weeks
    Explanation: Technically, a Critical Path has a Slack of zero. If the project is actually behind schedule, and the baseline date is still being used as the reference, the project could actually have negative Slack on the Critical Path. In this case, the negative Slack is twelve weeks.

7. Crosswind Custom Construction is building a shopping center. However, rain has delayed the finish by two weeks. The Project Manager is evaluating various ways to compress the schedule. The Project Manager suspects that the windows and climate control could occur at the same time instead of right after each other as laid out in the schedule. It is then discovered that local zoning laws will not allow this. This is an example of what?

    Correct Answer: (D) External Dependencies
    Explanation: An external dependency is that which is at the determination of something outside of the control of the Project Manager and team. A mandatory dependency is required and internal to the organization. The other answers are noise.

8. You and a fellow Project Manager are having a discussion about his project. He says the Network diagram for it has four paths that have the maximum duration of 25 units on the diagram. He says he doesn't have a Critical Path because they are all the same length, and you can only have one Critical Path. Which of the following is a true statement?

    Correct Answer: (B) You can have more than one Critical Path, but they are the longest paths on the project, and more than one Critical Path will increase your project risk.
    Explanation: The Critical Path is the longest path on the project. You can have more than one if the longest path on the network diagram is the same length. The more critical paths you have, the riskier the project is.

9. The Project Manager is creating an estimate for building a cellular infrastructure base station. It is something that is new to the Project Manager and his team. They decide to create a bottom-up estimate. All the following are advantages of this type of estimate except...

    Correct Answer: (C) It takes a great amount of time to create.
    Explanation: All the answers are characteristic of the bottom up estimate. Taking a great amount of time to create is not an advantage of the estimate.

10. The project team is working together on creating the plan for the data cleansing project. They have had some challenges associated with the planning. They are in the process of creating a Network diagram. What will this show the team?

    Correct Answer: (C) The sequencing of the tasks on the project
    Explanation: The Network diagram shows the sequencing of the tasks on the project. The Work Breakdown Structure (WBS) shows the Decomposition of the work of the project. The duration estimate of the project comes from the schedule.

11. The Project Manager is creating an estimate for building a warehouse and distribution center. It is a project similar to what he builds about 3 times a year. He is using the rule of thumb of $100 per square foot to calculate the estimate. What type of estimate is this?

Correct Answer: (A) Parametric
Explanation: The parametric estimate involves using a parameter of an amount per unit. In this case, $100 per square foot is the parameter. The analogous estimate is a top down estimate. The bottom up estimate is the detail that is created by the team. Gut feel is noise.

12. The road construction project is going well. There is a scope change adding four new exits and two additional lanes, as a result, a new team is brought in to assist the existing team in the new scope of the project. Upon arriving, the team asks to see where the project currently stands. What are they asking for?

Correct Answer: (B) Gantt chart
Explanation: The Gantt chart shows the people doing the work where the project is working to the plan. The Milestone chart is used for executive reporting. The Network diagram is used to show the sequencing of activities on the project. The Work Breakdown Structure (WBS) is used to show the work that is in the project.

13. The construction team is behind schedule on its project. The customer is considering giving the project to another company if they cannot get the project back on track. The team is considering putting more resources on the critical path to accelerate the schedule. This is an example of what?

Correct Answer: (B) Crashing
Explanation: Crashing is the process of putting more resources on the critical path items. Fast Tracking is re-sequencing the Critical Path activities to achieve schedule compression. Staff Acquisition doesn't fit here. Re-planning is noise.

14. The construction team is behind schedule on their project. The customer is considering giving the project to another company to complete if they cannot get the project back on track. The team is considering re-sequencing the Critical Path areas on the Network diagram to shorten the length of the schedule. This is an example of what?

Correct Answer: (C) Fast Tracking
Explanation: Fast Tracking is re-sequencing the Critical Path activities to achieve schedule compression. Crashing is the process of putting more resources on the critical items. Staff Acquisition doesn't fit here. Re-planning is noise.

15. Calculate the standard deviation for the following: Pessimistic=14, Optimistic=6, Realistic=8.

Correct Answer: (A) 1.33
Explanation: The formula for standard deviation is Pessimistic-Optimistic divided by 6.   The answer is 1.33.

16. You are putting together the final schedule on your security encryption project. The problem you are having is that you don't have a consistent usage of your resources. Some are working 2 hours a day, some 16 hours a day, and there are some days when they aren't scheduled to work at all. Which of the following below would fix this problem?

Correct Answer: (A) Resource Leveling
Explanation: Resource leveling takes peaks and valleys and levels them off for a consistent utilization of resources. Fast tracking and crashing are schedule compression techniques; those techniques solve a different type of problem. PERT analysis is noise in this question.

17. Which of the following utilizes a dummy?

Correct Answer: (A) Activity on Arrow (AOA)

Explanation: The dummy is used in an Activity on Arrow (AOA) diagram. Activity on Node (AON) doesn't use dummies. GERT and Gantt chart are noise in this question.

18. Which of the following would the team member use to determine the float on a project?

(A) Late Start-Early Start (LS-ES)
(B) Late Finish-Early Finish (LF-EF)
(C) A and B

Correct Answer: (C) A and B

Explanation: Float is calculated by subtracting either the early finish (EF) from the late finish (LF), or the early start (ES) from the late start (LS).

19. Crosswind Custom Websites is building an ecommerce system. However, conflicting priorities from other projects has delayed the finish by two weeks. The schedule shows that the next task is to define the requirements needed by the customer, then that is followed by the coding. This is an example of what?

Correct Answer: (D) Mandatory Dependencies

Explanation: A mandatory dependency is required and internal to the organization. The discretionary dependency is a dependency that the Project Manager can utilize options in completing or working with. Crashing and Lag are noise in this question.

20. The Project Manager is creating an estimate for a housing development. This is something for which he is quite experienced. The client needs the estimate in four hours. Which of the following types of estimates make the most sense to use?

Correct Answer: (D) Analogous

Explanation: The analogous estimate is also considered a top down estimate. It can be quickly created because it is based on expert knowledge of an area from previous projects. Parametric is an estimating technique that uses parameters, such as so much time per unit. A bottom up estimate is created by the team and can take time to create because of the details. Gut feel is noise.

21. You are the Project Manager on a merger and acquisition project. Task A (3 days) and Task B (4 days) can start immediately. Task C (2 days) can start after A and B are complete. Task D (5 days) can begin after task B is complete. Task E (6 days) can begin after task B is complete. Task F (4 days) can begin after tasks C and D are complete. Task G (5 days) can begin after tasks D and E are complete. Task H (4 days) can begin after tasks G and H are complete. What is the Critical Path?

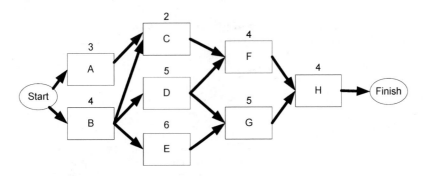

Correct Answer: (C) BEGH
Explanation: The Critical Path is the longest in the diagram. Of the five paths BEGH is the longest (19 days). BDGH (18 days), BDFH (17 days), BCFH (14 days), ACFH (13 days).

22. In the original Network diagram question, if Task D increases from five to eight days, what is the Critical Path, and what is the length?

Correct Answer: (B) BDGH, 21 days
Explanation: By increasing Task D from five days to eight days the path BDGH increases to twenty one days. This is the longest of the paths on the Network diagram.

23. Using the original Network diagram question, what is the Slack of Task D?

Correct Answer: (B) One day
Explanation: The longest path with Task D on it is path BDGH with a duration of 18 days. The Critical Path of BEGH is 19 days. Subtracting the length of BDGH from the Critical Path (19-18) shows a difference of one day. This is the Slack of Task D.

24. The construction team is building a new design for their company. This is a new design type at their company, and the market for the product is extremely unstable because of current interest rates. According to the site manager, a key to success will be to have an extremely accurate estimate on the resource needs for the project, because the company is resource constrained. Which type of duration estimating approach is the most accurate?

Correct Answer: (B) Bottom-up estimating
Explanation: Bottom-up estimating involves creating a very detailed, time consuming and accurate estimate as a result of working at the lowest level of the details of the work to create an estimate and rolling them up into a total overall estimate. Parametric estimating involves using a parameter such as $5.00 a square yard for material. Fast tracking involves re-sequencing already defined tasks to compress the overall duration of the schedule. Analogous estimating involves creating a relatively quick, high level estimate.

25. The auto manufacturing plant upgrade project is underway after some initial delays associated with the labor union approving the work. The labor union removes the workers from the project one day because the labor contract has been violated. They discover this was from a vendor requiring union personnel to do work that was not covered in the contract. Without this work being complete as needed, the project cannot continue. This is an example of what?

Correct Answer: (D) External dependency

Explanation: The External dependency is something outside the organization's control. The building inspector fits this criterion. The mandatory dependency is required and internal to the project. The discretionary dependency is at the option of the Project Manager and team. The city employee answer is noise.

26. Which of the following is the most accurate definition of a lag?

Correct Answer: (B) A delay inserted between tasks

Explanation: Lag is a delay between tasks on a Network diagram. An example is allowing a two-day delay after texturing a wall before painting it. This delay allows the wall texture to dry, but the drying time isn't a part of either task. The other three answers are associated with Slack.

27. Crosswind Custom Websites is building a huge ecommerce system. However, the designer getting sick has delayed the finish by two weeks. The Project Manager evaluates the schedule and determines that the graphics and backend work could occur at the same time instead of right after each other, as laid out in the schedule. This is an example of what?

Correct Answer: (B) Fast tracking

Explanation: Fast tracking involves re-sequencing of activities on the Network diagram to attain compression of the schedule. Crashing involves putting more resources on the Critical Path. Mandatory Dependencies involve a required predecessor before something can begin. Lag is a delay between tasks on the Network diagram.

28. Calculate the PERT estimate for the following: Pessimistic= 14, Optimistic= 6, Realistic= 8.

Correct Answer: (D) 8.66

Explanation: The PERT formula is (Pessimistic + Optimistic+ (4*Realistic)) divided by 6.   The answer is 8.66.

29. The housing development project is progressing well. The bank vice president who is the executive Sponsor gets promoted and moves to a new branch. His replacement is brought in from a new area and, upon arrival, asks to see where the project currently stands. Which of the following do you show him?

Correct Answer: (C) Milestone chart

Explanation: The Milestone chart is used for executive reporting. The Gantt chart shows the Project Team where the project is working to the plan. The Network diagram is used to show the sequencing of activities on the project. The Work Breakdown Structure (WBS) is used to show the work that is in the project.

30. Float on a Network diagram is also known as:

Correct Answer: (D) Slack

Explanation: Slack and Float are interchangeable terminology. Lag is a delay between tasks on a Network diagram. GERT and PERT are noise.

Cost

1. The project team is planning an upgrade to an electrical capacity for the manufacturing facility. During planning, the team members are confronted with the cost options for a new circuit that helps minimize the usage on the machinery. They consider the cost of purchasing the circuit for the time they need to develop the project. After that, the customer would take over the costs of the circuit. They are also considering a long-term commitment that the customer can make with the utility provider, which would provide a less costly solution over the use of the system. What type of analysis is the team considering?

   (A) Make-or-Buy analysis
   (B) Life Cycle Costing
   (C) Procurement Planning
   (D) Fixed Cost

2. Which of the following measurements would a Project Manager use to track the efficiency of the progress of the schedule?

   (A) Schedule Variance
   (B) Gantt chart
   (C) Variance Report
   (D) Schedule Performance Index

3. Task A is worth $400, is 95% complete, and actually cost $395. Task B is worth $350, is 90% complete, and actually cost $330 so far. Task C is worth $275, is 100% complete, and has cost $310 so far. The total budget is $2500. What is the Variance at Completion for the tasks listed?

   (A) $2668.09
   (B) $1633.09
   (C) -$168.09
   (D) $2500

4. The project is using a new auto press machine that cost $50,000 US. The Project Manager is told to set up depreciation for the server over a five-year schedule, with the auto press having a value of $0 at the end of five years. Standard depreciation will be used in the calculation. What is the amount per year the server will depreciate?

   (A) $2,500 US
   (B) Not enough information
   (C) $10,000 US
   (D) $5,000 US

5.   Company-wide access badges are an example of what type of project cost?

    (A) Variable
    (B) Variable indirect
    (C) Fixed direct
    (D) Fixed

6.   Task A is worth $400, is 95% complete, and actually cost $395. Task B is worth $350, is 90% complete, and actually cost $330 so far. Task C is worth $275, is 100% complete, and has cost $310 so far. The total budget is $2500. What is the Estimate at Completion for the tasks listed?

    (A) $2668.09
    (B) $2500
    (C) $1100.04
    (D) $690.63

7.   The project team members are reviewing the project management plan, focusing on the rules for reporting updates on the project. The majority of their tasks are less than two reporting periods long. Which of the following will they likely use?

    (A) Earned value
    (B) Forecast reporting
    (C) Fixed formula progress reporting
    (D) Weighted milestone

8.   The project is using some construction equipment to expand a parking facility at an athletic stadium. The finance department for the construction company explains that the equipment will be depreciated using the Double Declining Balance (DDB) format. This is an example of what?

    (A) Fixed Direct Cost
    (B) Standard Depreciation
    (C) Accelerated Depreciation
    (D) Fixed Cost

9.   The Project Manager has just received the charter. He is preparing an initial estimate called an order of magnitude (OOM) estimate. What is the range of an order of magnitude (OOM) estimate?

    (A) -5% to +10%
    (B) -10% to +5%
    (C) -300% to +75%
    (D) -25% to +75%

10. Task A is worth $400, is 95% complete, and actually cost $395. Task B is worth $350, is 90% complete, and actually cost $330 so far. Task C is worth $275, is 100% complete, and has cost $310 so far. The total budget is $2500. What is the Cost performance index for the tasks listed?

    (A) 0.937
    (B) 0.946
    (C) 1.16
    (D) 1.10

11. Task A is worth $400, is 95% complete, and actually cost $395. Task B is worth $350, is 90% complete, and actually cost $330 so far. Task C is worth $275, is 100% complete, and has cost $310 so far. The total budget is $2500. What is the Estimate to Complete for the tasks listed?

    (A) $2668.09
    (B) $1633.09
    (C) $970
    (D) $1025

12. The Project Manager and team are applying cost amounts to the pieces of the work packages and tasks. Which of the following processes are they performing?

    (A) Estimate Costs
    (B) Control Costs
    (C) Earned Value Management
    (D) Determine Budget

13. The project team is developing rules for reporting status on the project in the communications management plan. The majority of their tasks are greater than three reporting periods long. Which formats is best to use in this case.

    (A) Weighted milestone
    (B) Fixed formula progress reporting
    (C) Forecast reporting
    (D) Earned value

14. Task A is worth $200, is 100% complete, should have been done on day 1, and actually cost $200. Task B is worth $75, is 90% complete, should have been done on day 2, and actually cost $120 so far. Task C is worth $200, is 75% complete and should have been done on day 3, and has cost $175 so far. The total budget is $1000. What is the planned value as of day 1?

    (A) -$417.50
    (B) -$275.00
    (C) $495.00
    (D) $200.00

15. Task A is worth $400, is 95% complete, and actually cost $395. Task B is worth $350, is 90% complete, and actually cost $330 so far. Task C is worth $275, is 100% complete, and has cost $310 so far. The total budget is $2500. What is the Schedule Variance for the tasks listed?

    (A) -$55.00
    (B) -$65.00
    (C) 0.88
    (D) 0.84

16. Which of the following is an example of fixed formula status reporting?

    (A) PV multiplied by % Complete
    (B) Getting status updates from the project team
    (C) 0%/100% rule
    (D) The Project Manager updating the status reports quantitatively

17. The construction project is on schedule, but over budget. So far, $4M US has been spent on the project. The Sponsor is considering if it should allow the project to continue. What should it consider the $4M US that has been spent so far?

    (A) Sunk cost
    (B) The amount for phase 1
    (C) Opportunity cost
    (D) The budgeted cost of work performed

18. Project A has a NPV of $425K US over 2.5 years. Project B has an IRR of 9.2%. Project C has a BCR of 0.90:1. Project D has fourteen people on it and is encountering Scope creep and churn. Which of the following projects would stand the greatest chance of getting cancelled?

    (A) Project A
    (B) Project B
    (C) Project C
    (D) Project D

19. The electrical crew discovers that an additional circuit is needed to supply the appropriate electricity to the new injection molding machine at the plastic factory. This circuit will be used only on this machine, and only products from the kiwi product line will be made on the machine. What type of cost would this be to the product line?

    (A) Indirect
    (B) Direct
    (C) Indirect fixed
    (D) Variable

20. The project planning is progressing. But the team has become frustrated working with the accounting department to set up a system of codes that the accounting department will use to track work on the project. This is known as what?

    (A) Accounting codes
    (B) WBS numbering
    (C) Determine Budget
    (D) Chart of accounts

21. The project management team has performed earned value analysis on its project and discovered that the project is behind schedule and over budget. The SPI is 0.91 and the CPI is 0.62. The team is trying to determine how efficient it will need to be with the remaining resources on the project to complete the project on budget. Which of the following is the team trying to calculate?

    (A) Cost Variance
    (B) Cost Performance Index
    (C) Estimate to Complete
    (D) To Complete Performance Index

22. Project A has an NPV of $300K US over three years. Project B has an NPV of $530K US over six years. Project C has an NPV of $370K US over six years. Which of the following would you select?

    (A) Project A
    (B) Project B
    (C) Project C
    (D) Project A and C

23. The warehouse expansion project is in the middle of planning when the Project Manager presents a status reporting method to the team. It's called Earned Value Technique. To attain buy-in from the team, the Project Manager begins to explain what Earned Value status reporting can do for the project, explaining that it will measure which of the following?

    (A) Time and Cost
    (B) Scope, Time, and Cost
    (C) Scope and Cost
    (D) Scope and Time

24. Task A is worth $400, is 95% complete, and actually cost $395. Task B is worth $350, is 90% complete, and actually cost $330 so far. Task C is worth $275, is 100% complete, and has cost $310 so far. The total budget is $2500. What is the Cost Variance for the tasks listed?

    (A) -$65.00
    (B) -$55.00
    (C) 0.937
    (D) 0.946

25. Which of the following metrics would tell the Project Manager the status of the schedule on a project?

    (A) Cost Variance (CV)
    (B) Budget at Completion (BAC)
    (C) Schedule Performance Index (SPI)
    (D) Cost Performance Index (CPI)

26. Task A is worth $400, is 95% complete, and actually cost $395. Task B is worth $350, is 90% complete, and actually cost $330 so far. Task C is worth $275, is 100% complete, and has cost $310 so far. The total budget is $2500. What is the total Earned Value for the tasks listed?

    (A) -$970.00
    (B) $970.00
    (C) $1035.00
    (D) $1025

27. You have $2000 US today and can earn 12%. In future years, how much money will this be worth?

    (A) $1883 US
    (B) Not enough information
    (C) $2202 US
    (D) $2175 US

28. Which of the following two items are compared when evaluating the BCR on a project?

    (A) Revenue and profit
    (B) Profit margin
    (C) Benefit and profit
    (D) Revenue and cost

29. Which of the following measurements would the Project Manager use to show the remaining amount to be spent on the project based on current spending efficiency?

    (A) Cost Variance
    (B) Estimate to Complete
    (C) Estimate at Completion
    (D) Budget Remaining

30. The project planning is progressing. The team is using historical data and expert opinion to attempt to get a total price for the project. This process is known as what?

    (A) Analogous estimating
    (B) Estimate Costs
    (C) Determine Budget
    (D) Control Costs

Cost Answer Key

1. The project team is planning an upgrade to an electrical capacity for the manufacturing facility. During planning, the team members are confronted with the cost options for a new circuit that helps minimize the usage on the machinery. They consider the cost of purchasing the circuit for the time they need to develop the project. After that, the customer would take over the costs of the circuit. They are also considering a long-term commitment that the customer can make with the utility provider, which would provide a less costly solution over the use of the system. What type of analysis is the team considering?

    Correct Answer: (B) Life Cycle Costing
    Explanation: Life cycle costing involves looking at the long-term costs of something, instead of simply what it costs to create it. This can increase project costs but in the long run save the owner of the system money. The other three answers are noise.

2. Which of the following measurements would a Project Manager use to track the efficiency of the progress of the schedule?

    Correct Answer: (D) Schedule Performance Index
    Explanation: The Schedule Performance Index (SPI) shows the rate that the schedule is progressing compared to planned. For example, 1.0 means it is 100% according to plan; .8 means it is progressing at 80% of the rate planned; and 1.2 means it is progressing at 120% of the rate planned. Schedule Variance (SV) shows the amount ahead or behind schedule. The Gantt Chart is used by the PM and Team to graphically see what needs to be done on the project. The variance report shows the difference between baseline and actual performance.

3. Task A is worth $400, is 95% complete, and actually cost $395. Task B is worth $350, is 90% complete, and actually cost $330 so far. Task C is worth $275, is 100% complete, and has cost $310 so far. The total budget is $2500. What is the Variance at Completion for the tasks listed?

    Correct Answer: (C) -$168.09
    Explanation: The Variance at Completion (VAC) is the difference between the Budget at Completion (BAC) and the Estimate at Completion (ETC). To calculate this, subtract $2500 (BAC) from $2668.09 (EAC) for a difference of -$168.09 US.

4. The project is using a new auto press machine that cost $50,000 US. The Project Manager is told to set up depreciation for the server over a five-year schedule, with the auto press having a value of $0 at the end of five years. Standard depreciation will be used in the calculation. What is the amount per year the server will depreciate?

    Correct Answer: (C) $10,000 US
    Explanation: To calculate this, there are a few things to determine. What is the value of the asset at the end of the schedule? What is the amount of the asset to begin with? What is the number of years of the depreciation schedule? First, subtract the ending value of the asset from the beginning value of the asset ($50K-$0=$50K). The $50K is then divided by the years (5) of the depreciation schedule. This results in $10K per year of depreciation.

5. Company-wide access badges are an example of what type of project cost?

Correct Answer: (B) Variable indirect
Explanation: This type of cost would typically increase for every employee and will not likely be associated with a project. Therefore, Variable Indirect is the best description. Variable is not the best answer because Variable Indirect is a better solution. Fixed and fixed direct cost descriptions don't fit this type of cost.

6. Task A is worth $400, is 95% complete, and actually cost $395. Task B is worth $350, is 90% complete, and actually cost $330 so far. Task C is worth $275, is 100% complete, and has cost $310 so far. The total budget is $2500. What is the Estimate at Completion for the tasks listed?

Correct Answer: (A) $2668.09
Explanation: To calculate this, the CPI needs to be calculated first. To calculate the CPI, the Earned Value (EV) and Actual Cost (AC) need to be calculated first. To do this, multiply the percent complete of each task by its Planned Value (PV); that will provide the EV for each task. Sum the Earned Value of each task to determine the total Earned Value. Sum the Actual Cost of each task to determine the total Actual Cost. The Earned Value of $970.00 is then divided by the Actual Cost of $1035.00. This provides a CPI of 0.937. The BAC of $2500 is then divided by the CPI to produce an Estimated at Completion of $2668.09 US.

7. The project team members are reviewing the project management plan, focusing on the rules for reporting updates on the project. The majority of their tasks are less than two reporting periods long. Which of the following will they likely use?

Correct Answer: (C) Fixed formula progress reporting
Explanation: Fixed formula uses a partial credit approach such as 50/50 and is ideal when an activity is short, such as less than two reporting periods. The weighted milestone approach is ideal when an activity is over two reporting periods in length. Earned value shows the status of the scope, time and cost of the project. Forecast reporting focuses on what is getting ready to be done on the project.

8. The project is using some construction equipment to expand a parking facility at an athletic stadium. The finance department for the construction company explains that the equipment will be depreciated using the Double Declining Balance (DDB) format. This is an example of what?

Correct Answer: (C) Accelerated Depreciation
Explanation: Double Declining Balance (DDB) and sum of the digits are both examples of Accelerated Depreciation. DDB is not Standard Depreciation. The other two answers are noise.

9. The Project Manager has just received the charter. He is preparing an initial estimate called an order of magnitude (OOM) estimate. What is the range of an order of magnitude (OOM) estimate?

Correct Answer: (D) -25% to +75%
Explanation: The range of an order of magnitude (OOM) estimate is -25% to +75%. The Definitive Estimate has a range of -5% to +10%. The other two answers are noise in this question.

10. Task A is worth $400, is 95% complete, and actually cost $395. Task B is worth $350, is 90% complete, and actually cost $330 so far. Task C is worth $275, is 100% complete, and has cost $310 so far. The total budget is $2500. What is the Cost performance index for the tasks listed?

Correct Answer: (A) 0.937
Explanation: To calculate this, the Earned Value (EV) and Actual Cost (AC) need to be calculated first. To do this, multiply the percent complete of each task by its Planned Value (PV); that will provide the Earned Value (EV) for each task. Sum the Earned Value of each task to determine the total Earned Value. Sum the Actual Cost of each task to determine the total Actual Cost. The Earned Value of $970 is then divided by the Actual Cost of $1035. This provides a CPI of 0.937. This means that the project is getting $0.937 (or 94) cents value for every dollar it is spending.

11. Task A is worth $400, is 95% complete, and actually cost $395. Task B is worth $350, is 90% complete, and actually cost $330 so far. Task C is worth $275, is 100% complete, and has cost $310 so far. The total budget is $2500. What is the Estimate to Complete for the tasks listed?

Correct Answer: (B) $1633.09
Explanation: To calculate this, the Estimate at Completion (EAC) needs to be calculated first. To calculate the EAC, the Cost Performance Index (CPI) needs to be calculated first. To calculate the CPI, the Earned Value (EV) and Actual Cost (AC) need to be calculated first. To do this, multiply the percent complete of each task by its Planned Value (PV); that will provide the EV for each task. Sum the Earned Value of each task to determine the total Earned Value. Sum the Actual Cost of each task to determine the total Actual Cost. The Earned Value of $970 is then divided by the Actual Cost of $1035. This provides a CPI of 0.937. The BAC of $2500 is then divided by the CPI to produce an Estimated at Completion of $2668.09. The Estimate to Complete (ETC) is determined by subtracting the Actual Costs (AC) of $1035.00 from the Estimate at Completion (EAC) of $2668.09. The difference is $1633.09 US.

12. The Project Manager and team are applying cost amounts to the pieces of the work packages and tasks. Which of the following processes are they performing?

Correct Answer: (D) Determine Budget
Explanation: Determine Budget involves applying costs to the individual work packages or tasks. The Estimate Costs process involves getting a high level Cost Estimate for the overall project. Control Costs involves managing the costs of the project. Earned Value Management is noise.

13. The project team is developing rules for reporting status on the project in the communications management plan. The majority of their tasks are greater than three reporting periods long. Which formats is best to use in this case.

Correct Answer: (A) Weighted milestone
Explanation: The weighted milestone approach is ideal when an activity is over two reporting periods in length. Fixed formula uses a partial credit approach such as 50/50 and is ideal when an activity is short, such as less than two reporting periods. Earned value is used to show the status of the scope, time and cost of the project. Forecast reporting focuses on what is getting ready to be done on the project.

14. Task A is worth $200, is 100% complete, should have been done on day 1, and actually cost $200. Task B is worth $75, is 90% complete, should have been done on day 2, and actually cost $120 so far. Task C is worth $200, is 75% complete and should have been done on day 3, and has cost $175 so far. The total budget is $1000. What is the planned value as of day 1?

Correct Answer: (D) $200.00
Explanation: The planned value as of day one is $200.00. This value is generated by determining the planned value of Task A, which should have been done as of day 1 on the project.

15. Task A is worth $400, is 95% complete, and actually cost $395. Task B is worth $350, is 90% complete, and actually cost $330 so far. Task C is worth $275, is 100% complete, and has cost $310 so far. The total budget is $2500. What is the Schedule Variance for the tasks listed?

Correct Answer: (A) -$55.00
Explanation: To calculate this, the Earned Value (EV) and Planned Value (PV) need to be calculated first. To do this, multiply the percent complete of each task by its Planned Value (PV); that will provide the EV for each task. Sum the Earned Value of each task to determine the total Earned Value. Sum the Planned Value of each task (to date) to determine the total Planned Value. The Earned Value of $970.00 is then subtracted from the Planned Value of $1035.00. This provides a SV of -$55.00. This means that the project is $55.00 behind schedule.

16. Which of the following is an example of fixed formula status reporting?

Correct Answer: (C) 0%/100% rule
Explanation: The 0%/100% rule is an example of Fixed Formula Progress Reporting. It means that when the task starts, it is given 0% complete status and will not receive the 100% until it is complete. PV X % Complete is the formula for Earned Value. The other two answers are noise.

17. The construction project is on schedule, but over budget. So far, $4M US has been spent on the project. The Sponsor is considering if it should allow the project to continue. What should it consider the $4M US that has been spent so far?

Correct Answer: (A) Sunk cost
Explanation: Sunk costs are those that have already been spent on the project. They shouldn't be taken into consideration when determining whether to continue on the project. There is nothing in the situation about phasing the project. The budgeted cost of work performed is the Earned Value (EV). Opportunity cost doesn't apply here.

18. Project A has a NPV of $425K US over 2.5 years. Project B has an IRR of 9.2%. Project C has a BCR of 0.90:1. Project D has fourteen people on it and is encountering Scope creep and churn. Which of the following projects would stand the greatest chance of getting cancelled?

Correct Answer: (C) Project C
Explanation: Project C has a negative BCR in that it is creating less revenue than the costs. Project A and B have positive financials. Project D appears to have some issues, but we don't know enough about it to determine anything else.

19. The electrical crew discovers that an additional circuit is needed to supply the appropriate electricity to the new injection molding machine at the plastic factory. This circuit will be used only on this machine, and only products from the kiwi product line will be made on the machine. What type of cost would this be to the product line?

Correct Answer: (B) Direct
Explanation: The electric circuit is a direct cost. It is something purchased directly for the project or product. It is not an indirect or variable cost.

20. The project planning is progressing. But the team has become frustrated working with the accounting department to set up a system of codes that the accounting department will use to track work on the project. This is known as what?

Correct Answer: (D) Chart of accounts
Explanation: The Chart of Accounts sets up codes that are used to track project costs. The other three answers are noise.

21. The project management team has performed earned value analysis on its project and discovered that the project is behind schedule and over budget. The SPI is 0.91 and the CPI is 0.62. The team is trying to determine how efficient it will need to be with the remaining resources on the project to complete the project on budget. Which of the following is the team trying to calculate?

Correct Answer: (D) To Complete Performance Index
Explanation: The To Complete Performance Index (TCPI) shows the efficiency needed of the remaining resources to come in on budget. Cost variance (CV) shows the difference between work done and what was paid for it. Cost Performance Index (CPI) shows the ratio between the work done and what was paid for it. Estimate To Complete (ETC) shows the amount remaining to be spent based on the current spending efficiency (CPI).

22. Project A has an NPV of $300K US over three years. Project B has an NPV of $530K US over six years. Project C has an NPV of $370K US over six years. Which of the following would you select?

Correct Answer: (B) Project B
Explanation: Project B is the most attractive project because it has the highest dollar amount. The years listed with the NPV are noise as they are already factored into the dollar amount of the project. Project A and C are of less value than Project B.

23. The warehouse expansion project is in the middle of planning when the Project Manager presents a status reporting method to the team. It's called Earned Value Technique. To attain buy-in from the team, the Project Manager begins to explain what Earned Value status reporting can do for the project, explaining that it will measure which of the following?

Correct Answer: (B) Scope, Time, and Cost
Explanation: Earned value deals with Scope, Time and Cost. The Actual Cost (AC) shows cost. The Planned Value (PV) shows time. The Earned Value (EV) shows Scope. The formulas that work with these three variables show how the three are interacting together.

24. Task A is worth $400, is 95% complete, and actually cost $395. Task B is worth $350, is 90% complete, and actually cost $330 so far. Task C is worth $275, is 100% complete, and has cost $310 so far. The total budget is $2500. What is the Cost Variance for the tasks listed?

Correct Answer: (A) -$65.00
Explanation: To calculate this, the Earned Value (EV) and Actual Cost (AC) need to be calculated first. To do this, multiply the percent complete of each task by its Planned Value (PV); that will provide the EV for each task. Sum the Earned Value of each task to determine the total Earned Value. Sum the Actual Cost of each task to determine the total Actual Cost. The Earned Value of $970 is then subtracted from the Actual Cost of $1035. This provides a Cost Variance (CV) of -$65.00. This means that the project is $65.00 over budget.

25. Which of the following metrics would tell the Project Manager the status of the schedule on a project?

Correct Answer: (C) Schedule Performance Index (SPI)
Explanation: The Schedule Performance Index (SPI) will tell you if you are ahead, on, or behind schedule. Less than 1.0 means you are having schedule problems. 1.0 means you are doing exactly as planned on the schedule. Greater than 1.0 means you are progressing faster than planned. The Cost Performance Index (CPI) will show the spending efficiency of the project. The Budget at Completion (BAC) is the overall budget estimate for the project. The Cost Variance (CV) shows the amount that the project is over or under budget.

26. Task A is worth $400, is 95% complete, and actually cost $395. Task B is worth $350, is 90% complete, and actually cost $330 so far. Task C is worth $275, is 100% complete, and has cost $310 so far. The total budget is $2500. What is the total Earned Value for the tasks listed?

    Correct Answer: (B) $970.00
    Explanation: To calculate the Earned Value (EV), multiply the percent complete of each task by its Planned Value (PV); that will provide the EV for each task. The next step is to add the EV for each task to determine the total EV for the project. This amount is $970.00 US.

27. You have $2000 US today and can earn 12%. In future years, how much money will this be worth?

    Correct Answer: (B) Not enough information
    Explanation: To calculate Future Value (FV), you need to have a Present Value (PV), an interest rate, and the time period involved. Therefore, without a time period in the question, there is not enough information to answer the question.

28. Which of the following two items are compared when evaluating the BCR on a project?

    Correct Answer: (D) Revenue and cost
    Explanation: The BCR is the Benefit Cost Ratio. This considers the benefit (or revenue) and cost of an initiative. It doesn't factor in profit or profit margin.

29. Which of the following measurements would the Project Manager use to show the remaining amount to be spent on the project based on current spending efficiency?

    Correct Answer: (B) Estimate to Complete
    Explanation: The Estimate to Complete (ETC) is used to show the remaining amount of money expected to be needed based on current spending efficiency. This is calculated by subtracting Actual Costs (AC) from Estimate at Completion (EAC) which is EAC-AC=ETC. Budget remaining would not be applicable here because it wouldn't factor in spending efficiency.

30. The project planning is progressing. The team is using historical data and expert opinion to attempt to get a total price for the project. This process is known as what?

    Correct Answer: (B) Estimate Costs
    Explanation: The Estimate Costs process involves getting a high level Cost Estimate for the overall project. Determine Budget involves applying costs to the individual work packages or tasks. Control Costs involves managing the costs of the project. Analogous Estimating is noise.

Quality

1. The telephone company is building a new call center for its new Internet access division. Given that this is its first venture utilizing a call center, there are a number of new processes that will need to be created. Which of the following would show how to handle customers' various needs when they call the call center?

    (A) Checklist
    (B) Process flow
    (C) Control chart
    (D) Quality Audit

2. The project management team is trying to determine what is causing a problem on a project. They have isolated two variables from the information available to them. They suspect the problem is compounded by one variable impacting another. They want to see if there is a connection between the two variables. Which of the following will help them verify this?

    (A) Pareto diagram
    (B) Run chart
    (C) Scatter diagram
    (D) Control chart

3. You are doing quality planning on a project. The Sponsor puts into the Charter that the quality standard wanted on the project is +/- 3 Sigma. This translates to what %?

    (A) 50%
    (B) 99.73%
    (C) 68.26%
    (D) 95.46%

4. The company is in the scope verification phase of its project. It is tracking defects that come in from customers who are testing the project. Given the nature of a new project, they have a variety of defects that are being discovered. Organizing and prioritizing the defects is becoming a challenge and they want to be more proactive about it before it gets out of control. What would help them organize this better?

    (A) Flowchart
    (B) Pareto diagram
    (C) Fishbone diagram
    (D) Ishikawa diagram

5. The project is going through Quality Assurance. Which of the following is a key tool that the Project Manager will use in performing this work on the project?

    (A) Quality Audits
    (B) Quality improvement
    (C) Quality Management Plan
    (D) Quality testing

6. The Project Manager is evaluating data from a control chart and discovers nine consecutive data points on one side of the control chart. This is called what?

   (A) Too tight of control limits
   (B) A violation of the Seven Run Rule
   (C) Too loose of specification limits
   (D) Acceptable measurements

7. You are the Project Manager on a project that will improve the manufacturing process at your company. Quality has been a big issue because there has been an excessive amount spent on inventory with a lot of waste in the building process and return of product after it has been sold. Presently, the company has a 1 Sigma quality standard with its manufacturing process. There is a general belief that there are process issues behind this problem. Which of the following options looks like the best way to help create a more predictable outcome?

   (A) Increasing the quality to a Sigma level greater than 1
   (B) Utilizing a Fishbone diagram
   (C) Watching for violations of the Seven Run Rule
   (D) Making a greater use of checklists

8. The project is in the process of determining the accuracy of the work of the product. The project team members are utilizing a progressive elaboration approach. They discover that the process to measure the output is not going to produce the results needed. What process will fix the problem?

   (A) Plan Quality
   (B) Quality Management
   (C) Perform Quality Assurance
   (D) Perform Quality Control

9. The integrated circuit manufacturing process has been experiencing variance that is causing concern among the team. Some results have been within the specification limits, and some below the control tolerances. You want to learn more about the output of the process over the last six months. Which item below would show the most useful view of information?

   (A) Pareto diagram
   (B) Fishbone diagram
   (C) Run chart
   (D) Checklist

10. The team is in the process of planning what quality standards are needed on the project and how to achieve those standards. The team members are evaluating what could potentially cause issues in achieving these standards. Which of the following are they most likely to use to accomplish this goal?

    (A) Control chart
    (B) Fishbone diagram
    (C) Pareto diagram
    (D) Quality Audit

11. You are the Project Manager on a project that will improve your company's printing processes. Quality has been a big issue because there has been an excessive amount spent on inventory with much waste in the building process and disposal of printing that didn't meet the customer's needs. Presently, the company has a 3 Sigma quality standard with its printing process. There is talk of increasing the quality standard to help minimize these problems. Which of the following looks like the best way to increase the quality standard?

    (A) Making a greater use of checklists
    (B) Watching for violations of the Seven Run Rule
    (C) Utilizing a Fishbone diagram
    (D) Changing the quality to a Sigma level greater than 3

12. The Total Quality Management team is in the process of ensuring that the quality plan for the project will measure the product of the project as intended. What are the team members doing?

    (A) Quality Planning
    (B) Quality Control
    (C) Quality Audit
    (D) Quality Management

13. The bottling project is encountering a number of defects and needs to focus on what requires the most attention based on count. They want to have something that will graphically show this requirement plus a cumulative percentage of the defects. Which of the following would you use to provide this?

    (A) Pareto diagram
    (B) Ishikawa diagram
    (C) Fishbone diagram
    (D) Flowchart

14. The construction engineer is doing questionable work on his tasks on the remodeling project. The Project Manager has spoken to him about it a few times to no resolution. Functional Management has been made aware of this issue as well. Who is responsible for the quality of the work of the construction engineer?

    (A) The Construction Engineer
    (B) Project Manager
    (C) Senior Management
    (D) Functional Management

15. The printing company is putting a policy in place to use just-in-time manufacturing. It feels this policy will help minimize excess paper and ink costs and improve efficiency in processing and maximize square footage utilization. The amount of inventory needed for this type of process is what?

    (A) 25%
    (B) Minimal
    (C) Zero
    (D) Six Sigma

16. The Project Manager and a software developer are discussing quality. The Project Manager explains he just got back from PMP training based on the *PMBOK®* Guide - Fourth Edition. How will he define quality?

    (A) Meeting the customers needs
    (B) Scope verification
    (C) The degree to which a set of inherent characteristics fulfill requirements
    (D) Conformance to Use and Fitness of Requirements

17. The ecommerce project is in the middle of Quality Control. Which of the following is a tool that the Project Manager will use in this area?

    (A) Inspection
    (B) Quality management plan
    (C) Rework
    (D) Acceptance decisions

18. In quality control, the focus is on testing. Decisions should be made regarding how much testing is needed. Which of the following would be considered a negative associated with testing a sample instead of a population?

    (A) It is cheaper.
    (B) It is less destructive.
    (C) It is not very thorough.
    (D) It is quicker.

19. The Project Manager and a team member are discussing quality control and quality assurance. They are debating the differences between these two quality processes. What does Quality Assurance involve?

    (A) Verifying that the quality plan will help achieve the desired results
    (B) Defining the quality rules as they relate to the project
    (C) Keeping the customer happy
    (D) Measuring the output of the project

20. The Control chart has an upper control limit of ten and a lower control limit of four. What is the upper specification limit?

    (A) Greater than ten
    (B) Twelve
    (C) Less than four
    (D) Between ten and four

21. The company is implementing a quality improvement standard on its project work, trying to improve the culture to improve quality standards. The company views the need to shift the mentality of the company to a proactive approach to quality to achieve this objective. Which of the following would it not expect to deal with in an environment that has a proactive approach to quality?

    (A) Greater quality standard
    (B) Increased warranty support
    (C) Decreased warranty support
    (D) Less inventory needed

22. You are in the process of defining the quality standards for the project. You have defined the variables to measure and determined what attributes are important to you. Which of the following is not an attribute?

    (A) Height
    (B) Kilometers
    (C) Pounds
    (D) Feet

23. In evaluating the possibility of something happening versus not happening, the sum of all probabilities equals what?

    (A) 100
    (B) 1
    (C) 1 or 100%
    (D) 100%

24. You are the Project Manager on a project that will improve the manufacturing process at Router Computer company. Quality has been a big issue because there has been an excessive amount spent on inventory with a lot of waste in the building process and return of product after it has been sold. Presently, the company has a 2 Sigma quality standard with its manufacturing process. The quality team is presently evaluating options to improve quality at the company by trying to identify issues that could cause problems. Which of the following options looks like the best example of a quality tool for problem isolation?

    (A) Utilizing a Fishbone diagram
    (B) Watching for violations of the Seven Run Rule
    (C) Increasing the quality to a Sigma level greater than 2
    (D) Making a greater use of checklists

25. Who was the founder of Total Quality Management?

    (A) Deming
    (B) Herzberg
    (C) Ansoff
    (D) Johnson

26. Fishbone diagrams are also known as what?

    (A) Ishikawa diagram
    (B) Cause and Effect diagram
    (C) Cause/Effect diagram AND Ishikawa diagram
    (D) Pareto diagram

27. The project is progressing. As the company starts to release the product of the project to market, the consumer isn't buying it as the company had projected. This appears to be because in the past, the company has released products that had an excessive number of defects. Who was ultimately responsible for these products being released with the defects?

    (A) Functional Management
    (B) Project Manager
    (C) The developer
    (D) Senior Management

28. The networking company that won the procurement contract has begun development of the work of the project. Given that they are trying to get additional business with the customer, they are providing some extra features and functionality. Which of the following best describes this situation?

    (A) This is Gold Plating and it is a good thing to help them get more business.
    (B) This is Gold Plating and it is not a good practice.
    (C) This was an unsuccessful negotiation on the behalf of the company that won the contract.
    (D) This was a successful negotiation on the customer's behalf.

29. The company is having issues with quality on its projects. Senior Management has a mentality of dealing with problems when they absolutely need to instead of trying to eliminate them before they occur. The company would expect to work with all the following except...

    (A) Increased warranty support
    (B) Dissatisfied customers
    (C) More inventory needed
    (D) Training for process improvement

30. The bus driver for metro area rapid transit is in the process of driving the daily bus route. Adhering to the required startup process, the driver follows the procedures to ensure that he has properly selected and adjusted all the needed items to start up the bus for his route. Which of the following did he likely use?

    (A) Cause and Effect diagram
    (B) Company policy
    (C) Process flowchart
    (D) Checklist

Quality Answer Key

1. The telephone company is building a new call center for its new Internet access division. Given that this is its first venture utilizing a call center, there are a number of new processes that will need to be created. Which of the following would show how to handle customers' various needs when they call the call center?

   Correct Answer: (B) Process flow
   Explanation: The Process Flow will help define how company employees manage customers on the phone. A checklist is used to ensure certain things are done. A Control chart shows output over time. A Quality Audit is done to ensure that the quality standards of the project will be met.

2. The project management team is trying to determine what is causing a problem on a project. They have isolated two variables from the information available to them. They suspect the problem is compounded by one variable impacting another. They want to see if there is a connection between the two variables. Which of the following will help them verify this?

   Correct Answer: (C) Scatter diagram
   Explanation: The scatter diagram shows a relationship (or lack of a relationship) between two variables. The run chart (sometimes called a control chart) shows output over time. The Pareto diagram shows defects by quantity.

3. You are doing quality planning on a project. The Sponsor puts into the Charter that the quality standard wanted on the project is +/- 3 Sigma. This translates to what %?

   Correct Answer: (B) 99.73%
   Explanation: The percentage for 1 Sigma is 68.26%, 2 Sigma is 95.46%, 3 Sigma is 99.73%, and 50% is noise in this question.

4. The company is in the scope verification phase of its project. It is tracking defects that come in from customers who are testing the project. Given the nature of a new project, they have a variety of defects that are being discovered. Organizing and prioritizing the defects is becoming a challenge and they want to be more proactive about it before it gets out of control. What would help them organize this better?

   Correct Answer: (B) Pareto diagram
   Explanation: The Pareto diagram shows frequency of defects in a graphical format. The Flowchart shows process flow. Fishbone and Ishikawa are the same. They show what problems could happen or might be happening.

5. The project is going through Quality Assurance. Which of the following is a key tool that the Project Manager will use in performing this work on the project?

   Correct Answer: (A) Quality Audits
   Explanation: The Quality Audit is used in Quality Assurance to verify that the quality planning will meet the needs of the project. Quality improvement comes from Quality Control. Quality management plan is an output of Plan Quality. Quality testing is noise.

6. The Project Manager is evaluating data from a control chart and discovers nine consecutive data points on one side of the control chart. This is called what?

    Correct Answer: (B) A violation of the Seven Run Rule
    Explanation: The Seven Run Rule is a situation in which there are at least seven consecutive data points on one side of the mean, implying that the process could have some type of problem. The other three answers are noise.

7. You are the Project Manager on a project that will improve the manufacturing process at your company. Quality has been a big issue because there has been an excessive amount spent on inventory with a lot of waste in the building process and return of product after it has been sold. Presently, the company has a 1 Sigma quality standard with its manufacturing process. There is a general belief that there are process issues behind this problem. Which of the following options looks like the best way to help create a more predictable outcome?

    Correct Answer: (D) Making a greater use of checklists
    Explanation: Checklists allow the employee to attain a consistent process execution when followed. Assuming the checklist is sufficient and that the employee follows it, the process should possess a greater degree of stability. Fishbone diagrams work with problem isolation. Increasing the quality level will make a process more consistent, but it takes tools to do that. The checklist is a good quick fix that can have long term benefit, especially if the Sigma level is increased and higher quality expectations are put in place.

8. The project is in the process of determining the accuracy of the work of the product. The project team members are utilizing a progressive elaboration approach. They discover that the process to measure the output is not going to produce the results needed. What process will fix the problem?

    Correct Answer: (A) Plan Quality
    Explanation: The Plan Quality process would fix the problem. Quality Assurance and Quality Control are involved in this situation, but the solution comes in Plan Quality. Quality management is noise.

9. The integrated circuit manufacturing process has been experiencing variance that is causing concern among the team. Some results have been within the specification limits, and some below the control tolerances. You want to learn more about the output of the process over the last six months. Which item below would show the most useful view of information?

    Correct Answer: (C) Run chart
    Explanation: The Run chart's main purpose is to show output over time. This provides an opportunity to catch any trends and variance with the process. Fishbone diagrams are used for problem isolation. The Pareto diagram shows defects by count. A checklist is used to ensure consistency in doing something.

10. The team is in the process of planning what quality standards are needed on the project and how to achieve those standards. The team members are evaluating what could potentially cause issues in achieving these standards. Which of the following are they most likely to use to accomplish this goal?

    Correct Answer: (B) Fishbone diagram
    Explanation: The Fishbone diagram can be used to look for problems that could show up on the project. The Pareto diagram is used to show the frequency of defects. The Control chart shows output over time. A Quality Audit helps ensure that the project will meet the quality needs.

11. You are the Project Manager on a project that will improve your company's printing processes. Quality has been a big issue because there has been an excessive amount spent on inventory with much waste in the building process and disposal of printing that didn't meet the customer's needs. Presently, the company has a 3 Sigma quality standard with its printing process. There is talk of increasing the quality standard to help minimize these problems. Which of the following looks like the best way to increase the quality standard?

Correct Answer: (D) Changing the quality to a Sigma level greater than 3
Explanation: This is a tricky question. Some of the answers will potentially improve quality, but you are being asked what will increase the quality standard. Increasing the quality standard from 3 Sigma to 4 (or greater) Sigma will increase the quality standard.

12. The Total Quality Management team is in the process of ensuring that the quality plan for the project will measure the product of the project as intended. What are the team members doing?

Correct Answer: (C) Quality Audit
Explanation: The Quality Audit helps ensure that the quality management plan will meet the quality needs of the project. Quality Control deals with measuring the output of the project. Quality planning deals with defining the quality rules of the project. Quality management is noise.

13. The bottling project is encountering a number of defects and needs to focus on what requires the most attention based on count. They want to have something that will graphically show this requirement plus a cumulative percentage of the defects. Which of the following would you use to provide this?

Correct Answer: (A) Pareto diagram
Explanation: The Pareto diagram shows frequency of defects in a graphical format. The Flowchart shows process flow. Fishbone and Ishikawa are the same. They show what problems could happen, or might be happening.

14. The construction engineer is doing questionable work on his tasks on the remodeling project. The Project Manager has spoken to him about it a few times to no resolution. Functional Management has been made aware of this issue as well. Who is responsible for the quality of the work of the construction engineer?

Correct Answer: (A) The Construction Engineer
Explanation: The Construction Engineer is responsible for his own work. Senior Management is responsible for the quality of the company. The Project Manager is responsible for the quality on the project. Functional Management is noise.

15. The printing company is putting a policy in place to use just-in-time manufacturing. It feels this policy will help minimize excess paper and ink costs and improve efficiency in processing and maximize square footage utilization. The amount of inventory needed for this type of process is what?

Correct Answer: (C) Zero
Explanation: The amount of inventory needed for Just in Time (JIT) inventory is zero days. This implies that inventory arrives when it is needed.

16. The Project Manager and a software developer are discussing quality. The Project Manager explains he just got back from PMP training based on the *PMBOK® Guide - Fourth Edition*. How will he define quality?

Correct Answer: (C) The degree to which a set of inherent characteristics fulfill requirements

Explanation: The PMI Definition of Quality is the degree to which a set of inherent characteristics fulfill requirements, implying that you build what the requirements say should be built, and that the product built will perform and function as defined and needed.

17. The ecommerce project is in the middle of Quality Control. Which of the following is a tool that the Project Manager will use in this area?

Correct Answer: (A) Inspection

Explanation: Inspection is a key tool in Quality Control. It provides validation that the product was built as intended. A quality management plan is used to establish the standards and how to achieve them on the project. Rework comes when products are not built correctly. Acceptance decisions deal with defining what is and isn't acceptable.

18. In quality control, the focus is on testing. Decisions should be made regarding how much testing is needed. Which of the following would be considered a negative associated with testing a sample instead of a population?

Correct Answer: (C) It is not very thorough.

Explanation: It is not very thorough is a characteristic with testing a sample. Testing the population would be thorough because it tests everything; whereas, sample testing tests only a portion of the population.

19. The Project Manager and a team member are discussing quality control and quality assurance. They are debating the differences between these two quality processes. What does Quality Assurance involve?

Correct Answer: (A) Verifying that the quality plan will help achieve the desired results

Explanation: Quality Assurance involves ensuring that the quality plan will achieve the desired results of the project. Defining the quality rules as they relate to the project is in quality planning. Measuring the output of the project is Quality Control. Keeping the customer happy is noise.

20. The Control chart has an upper control limit of ten and a lower control limit of four. What is the upper specification limit?

Correct Answer: (A) Greater than ten

Explanation: The Upper Specification Limit (USL) is greater in value than the Upper Control Limit (UCL); therefore, with an Upper Control Limit of ten, the Upper Specification Limit would be greater than ten.

21. The company is implementing a quality improvement standard on its project work, trying to improve the culture to improve quality standards. The company views the need to shift the mentality of the company to a proactive approach to quality to achieve this objective. Which of the following would it not expect to deal with in an environment that has a proactive approach to quality?

Correct Answer: (B) Increased warranty support

Explanation: Typically, increased warranty support would not be encountered in an environment that has a proactive approach to quality. The other answers would be expected in an environment that proactively addresses quality.

22. You are in the process of defining the quality standards for the project. You have defined the variables to measure and determined what attributes are important to you. Which of the following is not an attribute?

Correct Answer: (A) Height
Explanation: Height is a variable. Something that you measure called a variable. The other three answers are attributes.

23. In evaluating the possibility of something happening versus not happening, the sum of all probabilities equals what?

Correct Answer: (C) 1 or 100%
Explanation: The sum of all probabilities is equal to 1 or 100%.

24. You are the Project Manager on a project that will improve the manufacturing process at Router Computer company. Quality has been a big issue because there has been an excessive amount spent on inventory with a lot of waste in the building process and return of product after it has been sold. Presently, the company has a 2 Sigma quality standard with its manufacturing process. The quality team is presently evaluating options to improve quality at the company by trying to identify issues that could cause problems. Which of the following options looks like the best example of a quality tool for problem isolation?

Correct Answer: (A) Utilizing a Fishbone diagram.
Explanation: The Fishbone diagram is a quality tool that can be used to look for the source or root cause of other symptoms you might be experiencing in an area. The Seven Run Rule can occur on a Control chart when looking at output over time. Increasing the quality level is not a tool nor will it isolate a problem. A checklist could be used as a tool but won't help isolate problems.

25. Who was the founder of Total Quality Management?

Correct Answer: (A) Deming
Explanation: Dr. Deming was the father of Total Quality Management (TQM). Herzberg was associated with Theory X and Y. Ansoff is a strategic management methodologist. Johnson is the author of this book.

26. Fishbone diagrams are also known as what?

Correct Answer: (C) Cause/Effect diagram AND Ishikawa diagram
Explanation: Fishbone diagrams are known as both Cause/Effect diagrams AND Ishikawa diagrams. Pareto deals with showing frequency of defects.

27. The project is progressing. As the company starts to release the product of the project to market, the consumer isn't buying it as the company had projected. This appears to be because in the past, the company has released products that had an excessive number of defects. Who was ultimately responsible for these products being released with the defects?

Correct Answer: (D) Senior Management
Explanation: Senior Management is responsible for the quality of the company. The developer is responsible for his own work. The Project Manager is responsible for the quality on the project. Functional Management is noise.

28. The networking company that won the procurement contract has begun development of the work of the project. Given that they are trying to get additional business with the customer, they are providing some extra features and functionality. Which of the following best describes this situation?

Correct Answer: (B) This is Gold Plating and it is not a good practice.
Explanation: Gold Plating is what is happening here. It is not good by any means because you should provide customers what they want and nothing more or less. Negotiations have nothing to do this situation.

29. The company is having issues with quality on its projects. Senior Management has a mentality of dealing with problems when they absolutely need to instead of trying to eliminate them before they occur. The company would expect to work with all the following except…

Correct Answer: (D) Training for process improvement
Explanation: Training for process improvement is something that a company with a proactive approach to quality will do. The other answers deal with the reactive (nonconformance) environment described in the situation.

30. The bus driver for metro area rapid transit is in the process of driving the daily bus route. Adhering to the required startup process, the driver follows the procedures to ensure that he has properly selected and adjusted all the needed items to start up the bus for his route. Which of the following did he likely use?

Correct Answer: (D) Checklist
Explanation: The checklist can provide assistance in ensuring that certain steps that need to be completed are done as planned. The Process Flowchart shows how activities flow. Cause and Effect diagram is used for problem planning and solving. Company policy is noise.

Human Resources

1. The Project Manager has some issues on the team between three team members with different solutions to a critical path related problem. What is the best method to resolve the conflict?

    (A) Problem solving
    (B) Reward
    (C) Withdrawal
    (D) Compromise

2. The Project Manager is involved in Human Resources Planning on a project. All the following would expect to be created except...

    (A) Team development
    (B) Role and responsibility assignments
    (C) Staffing management plan
    (D) Organizational chart

3. The Project Manager tells a team member on the project that she can attend some training for a new computer program. He further explains that this new skill will be used by the company in the future. He lets the team member know that he approved this training because of the good work the team member has done on the project. This is an example of what type of power?

    (A) Formal
    (B) Reward
    (C) Award
    (D) Compromise

4. The Project Manager has created the staffing plan and will be starting the project soon. Resumes are being reviewed, and interviewing will be starting soon for external candidates. The lead candidate for the senior programming position has been offered a position. What process is the Project Manager involved in?

    (A) Developing the Project Team
    (B) Acquire Project Team
    (C) Resource requirements
    (D) Hiring and interviewing

5. A Responsibility Assignment Matrix would eliminate which of the following?

    (A) Confusion on how long the tasks are
    (B) Confusion on who is on the team
    (C) Confusion on what order tasks come in
    (D) Confusion on who is responsible for doing what

6.   The project is in a Balanced Matrix environment. There are significant challenges with the schedule and resource constraints of the project. Project personnel have been complaining to the Project Manager about the environment. In this type of environment, who controls the resources?

(A) Project Manager
(B) Functional Manager
(C) Senior Management
(D) Project Coordinator

7.   In performing Human Resources Management on a project, an organizational breakdown structure (OBS) is also known as what?

(A) Staffing Management Plan
(B) Organizational chart
(C) Resource Histogram
(D) Responsibility Assignment Matrix

8.   The Project Manager is in the process of planning the project. The company wants to ensure the team members know who is accountable for completion of various tasks and processes associated with the projects. What document can he include in the Project Management Plan that will help eliminate this problem?

(A) Organization Chart
(B) Responsibility Assignment Matrix
(C) Gantt Chart
(D) Staffing Plan

9.   The construction project has some challenges. The Project Manager has continually had to tell the team what to do. The team members also do not seem to trust management that much and often appear unmotivated. This is an example of what?

(A) Theory X environment
(B) Bad performance
(C) Theory Y environment
(D) Forcing

10.   The team is going through some resource over-utilization issues on the project. The linemen are working excessive hours installing electrical and data communication lines. The Project Manager has gone back to planning to re-evaluate the situation. Which of the following can provide help in seeing how serious the issue is?

(A) Pareto diagram
(B) Control chart
(C) Staffing Management Plan
(D) Resource Histogram

11. The project has been very trying on a lot of people. There are some key team members considering leaving the project and taking jobs at a new startup company. Which of the following would be a key motivator to keep them on the project?

    (A) Theory Y motivation strategy
    (B) Compromise
    (C) Fringe benefits
    (D) Perks

12. The Project Manager is involved planning a real estate project for a big land development. There have been a number of resource issues so far on the project. The Project Manager is evaluating what was used in establishing the management of the project team. All the following should be considered for managing the project team except...

    (A) Work Performance Information
    (B) Project Staff Assignments
    (C) Ground Rules
    (D) Project Organization Charts

13. Which of the following is not likely a project resource for a software project?

    (A) Conference room near the team location
    (B) Project Manager
    (C) Functional manager
    (D) Computer programmer

14. Which of the following is not a level in Maslow's Hierarchy of Needs?

    (A) Psychedelic
    (B) Belonging
    (C) Esteem
    (D) Safety

15. The project has gone well without any significant issues. The team appears to be fairly self motivated and working toward verifying scope and formal acceptance. Some of the team members are having a discussion about how much fun the work has been as well. Which of the following best describes this environment?

    (A) Theory Y environment
    (B) Theory X environment
    (C) Motivation theory
    (D) Reward theory

16. The Project Manager is having issues with a key team member meeting deadlines. The team member has a sensitive personality that doesn't deal with issues well, but the project cannot slip because of this either. What type of Conflict Resolution technique will have the worst impact with the team member?

    (A) Forcing
    (B) Formal
    (C) Penalty
    (D) Smoothing

17. The Project Coordinator is in charge of planning the semester classes at the annual quality congress. She is trying to allocate various resource types to work together such as instructors, rooms, audio/video equipment for the various events associated with the event. Which of the following is she most likely to use to show this information?

    (A) Resource breakdown structure
    (B) Organizational chart
    (C) Responsibility assignment matrix
    (D) Risk breakdown structure

18. The architect has recently been promoted from lead architect to department manager. In this new position, he will be responsible for managing projects and project resources. Over the five years he has been with the company, he was always ranked as one of the top architects but has had no formal Project Management training. This is an example of what?

    (A) Reward power
    (B) Halo Theory
    (C) Equal opportunity employment
    (D) Problem solving

19. The bank software project has a number of key Stakeholders who have provided input to the direction of the project. Which of the following best describes a Stakeholder on a project?

    (A) Stockholders of the company
    (B) Someone who is impacted by the project
    (C) Functional Management
    (D) Senior Management

20. The Project Manager is focusing on the evolution of the project team into a well performing organization. He is focusing on turning the group of people into a well performing work team. When does this occur in a project?

    (A) During execution
    (B) During planning
    (C) During off hours events
    (D) Throughout the project

21. Two important project team members are disagreeing about a potential solution. The Project Manager gets involved and tries to remind them of how they have worked together before and created great results. This is an example of what type of Conflict Resolution?

    (A) Smoothing
    (B) Compromise
    (C) Referent
    (D) Withdrawal

22. What will the Project Manager create as a result of creating the project team?

    (A) Performance improvements
    (B) Team-building activities
    (C) Smoothing
    (D) The team becoming friends after the project is complete

23. The senior Project Manager at the company is helping look out for a newer Project Manager who is working on another project. They meet every few days to see how the newer Project Manager's project is performing as well as discussing concepts that should help make the less experienced Project Manager more experienced. This is an example of what?

    (A) Mentoring
    (B) Forcing
    (C) Motivational Theory
    (D) An intern program

24. The Project Manager is planning how many people he will need on the construction project. This will more than likely require more than one person with each skill set. He is reviewing the level of effort of each skill set needed each month on the project. What will he likely use to visually represent this data?

    (A) Responsibility Assignment Matrix (RAM)
    (B) Resource Histogram
    (C) Pareto diagram
    (D) PERT chart

25. The Project Manager just received an industry award for her recent work. The current project is a new version of her last project. What type of power will the Project Manager utilize for the best results on the project?

    (A) Referent
    (B) Compromise
    (C) Formal
    (D) Expert

26. All the following are examples of developing the project team except...

   (A) Attending a sporting event as a group
   (B) Performance reviews
   (C) A team lunch
   (D) Creating the WBS of the project

27. The project is progressing well but has begun to experience resource conflicts with people who are being pulled from the project by Functional management for other work. What role will typically help resolve these resource issues?

   (A) Functional Management
   (B) Senior Management
   (C) Sponsor
   (D) Project Management

28. The Project Manager is assigned to a new project. She is using a responsibility assignment matrix (RAM) after recently attending a project management training class. What benefit will this provide to her on the project?

   (A) Who does what work and when they are to do it
   (B) Information about who is responsible for what work
   (C) What sequence the resources are to perform the tasks in
   (D) At what location the work is done

29. In the performance of human resources functions on a project, which of the following is not a process that would be done by the Project Manager?

   (A) Develop Human Resource Plan
   (B) Team motivation
   (C) Develop Project Team
   (D) Acquire Project Team

30. The sponsor has just signed the charter. What type of power does the Project Manager have as a result of this?

   (A) Formal
   (B) Reward
   (C) Problem solving
   (D) Referent

Human Resources Answer Key

1.   The Project Manager has some issues on the team between three team members with different solutions to a critical path related problem. What is the best method to resolve the conflict?

   Correct Answer: (A) Problem solving
   Explanation: Problem solving is the most proactive and lasting solution. Reward really wouldn't fit here as it is a type of power. Compromise could water down the solution. Withdrawing would be professionally irresponsible.

2.   The Project Manager is involved in Human Resources Planning on a project. All the following would expect to be created except…

   Correct Answer: (A) Team development
   Explanation: Team development would have to occur after the organizational planning, because there wouldn't be even the basic definition of the team until that point.

3.   The Project Manager tells a team member on the project that she can attend some training for a new computer program. He further explains that this new skill will be used by the company in the future. He lets the team member know that he approved this training because of the good work the team member has done on the project. This is an example of what type of power?

   Correct Answer: (B) Reward
   Explanation: The Reward power comes from the Project Manager's ability to reward an employee for good work. Formal is the type of power that is derived from the Charter for the Project Manager. Compromise is a conflict resolution that involves everyone giving a little to attain a solution. Award is noise.

4.   The Project Manager has created the staffing plan and will be starting the project soon. Resumes are being reviewed, and interviewing will be starting soon for external candidates. The lead candidate for the senior programming position has been offered a position. What process is the Project Manager involved in?

   Correct Answer: (B) Acquire Project Team
   Explanation: Acquiring the project team involves getting people on the project. Resource requirements would already have been defined before the interviewing started. Developing the project team should happen after acquiring the project team is complete. Hiring and interviewing is noise.

5.   A Responsibility Assignment Matrix would eliminate which of the following?

   Correct Answer: (D) Confusion on who is responsible for doing what
   Explanation: The Responsibility Assignment Matrix shows who is responsible for what areas on the project. The Network diagram would provide guidance on what order the tasks occur. The organizational structure would confirm who is on the team, and what the reporting structure is. The Gantt chart or schedule will show how long the tasks are.

6.   The project is in a Balanced Matrix environment. There are significant challenges with the schedule and resource constraints of the project. Project personnel have been complaining to the Project Manager about the environment. In this type of environment, who controls the resources?

Correct Answer: (B) Functional Manager

Explanation: In a Matrix Environment, the Functional Manager traditionally will control the resources. The Project Manager will have those resources available for project work as the Functional Manager sees necessary. Senior Management will help resolve resource conflicts. The Project Coordinator is noise.

7.   In the performance of Human Resources Management on a project, an organizational breakdown structure (OBS) is also known as what?

Correct Answer: (B) Organizational chart

Explanation: The Organizational Breakdown Structure (OBS) is also known as an organizational chart. The Staffing Management Plan defines the staffing rules as it relates to the project. The Responsibility Assignment Matrix shows who is responsible for what on the project. The Resource Histogram shows what quantities of resources are utilized over time.

8.   The Project Manager is in the process of planning the project. The company wants to ensure the team members know who is accountable for completion of various tasks and processes associated with the projects. What document can he include in the Project Management Plan that will help eliminate this problem?

Correct Answer: (B) Responsibility Assignment Matrix

Explanation: The RAM shows who is responsible for what on the project. The Gantt chart shows when tasks are done. The staffing plan addresses the staffing related needs of the project. The Organization chart shows how the organization is structured.

9.   The construction project has some challenges. The Project Manager has continually had to tell the team what to do. The team members also do not seem to trust management that much and often appear unmotivated. This is an example of what?

Correct Answer: (A) Theory X environment

Explanation: A theory X environment typically will have employees having to be told what to do, having distrust for management, and lacking motivation. Theory Y is the opposite. The other two answers are noise.

10. The team is going through some resource over-utilization issues on the project. The linemen are working excessive hours installing electrical and data communication lines. The Project Manager has gone back to planning to re-evaluate the situation. Which of the following can provide help in seeing how serious the issue is?

Correct Answer: (D) Resource Histogram

Explanation: The Resource Histogram displays how resources are utilized on the project. It can be displayed a number of ways, but the general view shows some criteria of resources on the project over a time scale. The Control chart shows output over time. The Pareto diagram shows frequency of defects. The Staffing Management Plan addresses how to deal with staffing related items on the project.

11. The project has been very trying on a lot of people. There are some key team members considering leaving the project and taking jobs at a new startup company. Which of the following would be a key motivator to keep them on the project?

Correct Answer: (D) Perks
Explanation: Perks are benefits that are not available to everyone. These are items that might keep people on this project, because the perks might not be available if they go to another area to work. Fringe benefits are benefits that everyone gets; therefore, they shouldn't be a motivator. Theory Y and compromise are noise.

12. The Project Manager is involved planning a real estate project for a big land development. There have been a number of resource issues so far on the project. The Project Manager is evaluating what was used in establishing the management of the project team. All the following should be considered for managing the project team except…

Correct Answer: (C) Ground Rules
Explanation: Ground rules are established in developing the project team. The other three processes are inputs to managing the project team. Project staff assignment helps establish who is on the team. Work performance information provides details as to what work is being done and the project organization chart displays organization structure and reporting relationships.

13. Which of the following is not likely a project resource for a software project?

Correct Answer: (C) Functional manager
Explanation: Resources can be anything that helps contribute to a project's success. No disrespect toward Functional Managers, but the other answers are clearly better examples of project resources that are used directly on a project. The functional manager might be involved in the project but usually in only controlling resources.

14. Which of the following is not a level in Maslow's Hierarchy of Needs?

Correct Answer: (A) Psychedelic
Explanation: The levels of Maslow's Hierarchy of Needs are Physiological, Safety, Belonging, Esteem, and Self Actualization.

15. The project has gone well without any significant issues. The team appears to be fairly self motivated and working toward verifying scope and formal acceptance. Some of the team members are having a discussion about how much fun the work has been as well. Which of the following best describes this environment?

Correct Answer: (A) Theory Y environment
Explanation: A theory Y environment usually involves people who are motivated and can work with an end goal in mind, instead of being told what to do. They also do not require much supervision and tend to enjoy their work. A theory X environment is usually the opposite type of environment. Motivation theory and reward theory are noise.

16. The Project Manager is having issues with a key team member meeting deadlines. The team member has a sensitive personality that doesn't deal with issues well, but the project cannot slip because of this either. What type of Conflict Resolution technique will have the worst impact with the team member?

Correct Answer: (A) Forcing
Explanation: Forcing people to do something they don't want to do will have the worst long-term impact on the team. Smoothing is not as bad as forcing. Formal and penalty are types of power that the Project Manager has.

17. The Project Coordinator is in charge of planning the semester classes at the annual quality congress. She is trying to allocate various resource types to work together such as instructors, rooms, audio/video equipment for the various events associated with the event. Which of the following is she most likely to use to show this information?

Correct Answer: (A) Resource breakdown structure
Explanation: The Resource Breakdown Structure will show resource utilization across the organization regardless of what division or group they report to. This works well for various resource types described above. The Organizational Chart shows who or what position reports to what person or position on the project. The Risk Breakdown Structure shows a decomposition of the potential risks on the project. The Responsibility Assignment Matrix shows who is responsible for what on the project.

18. The architect has recently been promoted from lead architect to department manager. In this new position, he will be responsible for managing projects and project resources. Over the five years he has been with the company, he was always ranked as one of the top architects but has had no formal Project Management training. This is an example of what?

Correct Answer: (B) Halo Theory
Explanation: The Halo Theory implies that because people are good at their current jobs, they would be good at Project Management regardless of their background or training. The other three answers are noise.

19. The bank software project has a number of key Stakeholders who have provided input to the direction of the project. Which of the following best describes a Stakeholder on a project?

Correct Answer: (B) Someone who is impacted by the project
Explanation: The Stakeholder is someone who is impacted by the work of the project. That can include stockholders, Senior Management, and Functional Management.

20. The Project Manager is focusing on the evolution of the project team into a well performing organization. He is focusing on turning the group of people into a well performing work team. When does this occur in a project?

Correct Answer: (A) During execution
Explanation: Team-building occurs in execution of the project management plan. Planning creates the project management plan, executing the work of the Project Management Plan starts the team development if it wasn't already started in planning.

21. Two important project team members are disagreeing about a potential solution. The Project Manager gets involved and tries to remind them of how they have worked together before and created great results. This is an example of what type of Conflict Resolution?

Correct Answer: (A) Smoothing
Explanation: Smoothing involves trying to minimize the conflict on the project and remember things that have worked well. Compromise involves everyone conceding a little to come up with a solution. Referent is name dropping or political alignment for power. Withdrawal is stepping away and ignoring the problem, which would be professionally irresponsible.

22. What will the Project Manager create as a result of creating the project team?

Correct Answer: (A) Performance improvements
Explanation: Developing the project team can happen throughout the project. Generally speaking, it will take a group of people and turn them into a team resulting in performance improvement. Team-building activities would actually happen during developing the project team. The other two answers are noise.

23. The senior Project Manager at the company is helping look out for a newer Project Manager who is working on another project. They meet every few days to see how the newer Project Manager's project is performing as well as discussing concepts that should help make the less experienced Project Manager more experienced. This is an example of what?

Correct Answer: (A) Mentoring
Explanation: Mentoring is a process in which someone more experienced helps tutor someone not as experienced in the field of choice. An intern program doesn't exactly fit in this case. The other two answers are noise.

24. The Project Manager is planning how many people he will need on the construction project. This will more than likely require more than one person with each skill set. He is reviewing the level of effort of each skill set needed each month on the project. What will he likely use to visually represent this data?

Correct Answer: (B) Resource Histogram
Explanation: The Resource Histogram will show how certain resources are utilized over time. The Responsibility Assignment Matrix shows who is responsible for what area of the project. The Pareto diagram shows defects in frequency of occurrence. The PERT chart is noise.

25. The Project Manager just received an industry award for her recent work. The current project is a new version of her last project. What type of power will the Project Manager utilize for the best results on the project?

Correct Answer: (D) Expert
Explanation: Expert power implies that the person is bringing some type of specific knowledge to the area or project. Formal power would come from the charter. Referent power deals with whom you know in the organization. Compromise is noise, as it is a conflict resolution technique.

26. All the following are examples of developing the project team except…

Correct Answer: (B) Performance reviews
Explanation: Performance reviews are not a team-building event. Such a review is the process during which an employee and supervisor review project performance. Team-building involves the group of people on the project forming into a cohesive whole.

27. The project is progressing well but has begun to experience resource conflicts with people who are being pulled from the project by Functional management for other work. What role will typically help resolve these resource issues?

Correct Answer: (B) Senior Management
Explanation: Typically, most environments are somewhere between Functional and Projectized. That being the case, the matrix environments will typically have a Functional Manager controlling resources. This can lead to conflict between the Project Manager and Functional Managers. Senior Management is usually the entity that resolves these conflicts. The Sponsor traditionally gets involved when there is money. Functional Management is noise.

28. The Project Manager is assigned to a new project. She is using a responsibility assignment matrix (RAM) after recently attending a project management training class. What benefit will this provide to her on the project?

Correct Answer: (B) Information about who is responsible for what work
Explanation: The Responsibility Assignment Matrix shows who is responsible for what work on the project. The Gantt chart shows who does what work and when they are to do it. The Network diagram provides the sequence that the resources are to perform the tasks in. At what location the work is done is noise.

29. In the performance of human resources functions on a project, which of the following is not a process that would be done by the Project Manager?

Correct Answer: (B) Team motivation

Explanation: The four human resources processes are Develop Human Resource Plan, Acquire Project Team, Develop Project Team, and Manage Project Team.

30. The sponsor has just signed the charter. What type of power does the Project Manager have as a result of this?

Correct Answer: (A) Formal

Explanation: Once the Charter is signed, the Project Manager has formal authority. The level of authority is defined in the Charter. Reward Power involves providing incentives to people on the project. Referent Power involves whom you are connected to on the project or in the organization. The other answer is noise.

Communications

1. What type of report would the team member read to show what was completed in the last month on the project?

    (A) Progress Report
    (B) Variance Report
    (C) Status Report
    (D) Earned Value Report

2. In the user of the communications model, all the following would be considered by the Project Manager except...

    (A) Sender
    (B) Receiver
    (C) Language
    (D) Message

3. The Project Manager has been working with six influential stakeholders to determine their communication requirements. All the following could be expected as communication requirements on a project except...

    (A) The name of the human resources manager for the company
    (B) Names and contact information for the members of the project change control board
    (C) Steps to take regarding a project change request
    (D) Project status meeting time and location

4. You are the Project Manager on a medical project. You have been analyzing project data from the last two week reporting period. The main data you have been looking at involves the value of the work that should have been done, what was done, and what was paid for it. What type of report format are you looking at?

    (A) Progress report
    (B) Status report
    (C) Performance report
    (D) Variance report

5. You are the Project Manager for a global point of sale upgrade project that is utilizing an offshore development company. There have been a number of communication challenges with misinterpretation of requirements and failure to follow through with things associated with the store rollout that the Project Manager felt needed attention. What type of communication would help improve these problems?

    (A) Verbal
    (B) Informal Verbal
    (C) Formal Written
    (D) Formal

6. The Project Manager is planning the project. He is meeting with project stakeholders to determine their communication needs for the project. He is finding out what type of information they need, when it is needed, and in what format. When done this will be added to the Project Management Plan. What will he create as a result of this work?

    (A) Staffing plan
    (B) Information Distribution Plan
    (C) Team list
    (D) Communication Management Plan

7. What type of report would the Project Manager use to compare what has been completed to what was scheduled to be done?

    (A) Earned Value Report
    (B) Status Report
    (C) Variance Report
    (D) Progress Report

8. The Project Manager is reporting performance on a project to the stakeholders. She is reporting status on the scope, cost, and schedule of the project. What type of report is this?

    (A) Earned Value Report
    (B) Status Report
    (C) Variance Report
    (D) Progress Report

9. What type of report will the Project Manager use to see what has been completed so far on the software project?

    (A) Earned Value Report
    (B) Status Report
    (C) Variance Report
    (D) Progress Report

10. Which of the following would a Project Manager need to create a project progress report?

    (A) Work results
    (B) Change Request
    (C) Project archives
    (D) Status reports

11. The Project Manager has just created with the team a decomposition of the work of the project. This will aid in determining resource needs, how long the project should take and how much it should cost. What did they create?

    (A) Gantt chart
    (B) Schedule
    (C) Responsibility Assignment Matrix
    (D) Work Breakdown Structure

12. In the communication model, if the Project Manager is communicating to the receiver which of the following will they focus on delivering and ensuring that it can be decoded correctly?

(A) Medium
(B) Feedback
(C) Message
(D) Noise

13. All the following could be considered mediums for communication by a project team member except…

(A) Staff meetings
(B) Email
(C) Message
(D) Video conference

14. All the following are examples of communication infrastructure that a Project Manager could encounter on a project except…

(A) Conference rooms
(B) Spreadsheet applications
(C) Intranet site
(D) E-mail system

15. The Charter on a project would be viewed as what type of communication?

(A) Formal
(B) Formal Written
(C) Contract
(D) Verbal

16. The Project Manager has a project team that can never keep a meeting on track because it always ends up off topic and running longer than anticipated with people bringing up side items and out of scope topics. Which of the following would improve the meetings?

(A) Create and publish an agenda, and establish the leader of the meeting
(B) Create and publish an agenda
(C) Determine who is in charge of the meeting
(D) Send the team to communication training

17. Which of the following does the Project Manager and team need to begin creating the Communications Management Plan?

(A) Formal communication
(B) Communication infrastructure
(C) Project Scope Statement
(D) Stakeholder analysis

18. The Project Manager spends a lot of time replying to email and meeting with stakeholders about the execution of the project. How much of a Project Manager's job is spent communicating?

    (A) 100%
    (B) 60+ hours a week
    (C) 40 hours a week
    (D) Approximately 90%

19. The Project Manager is determining what the stakeholder communication needs of the project are. What will he have completed when he is done with this part of planning?

    (A) Stakeholder Analysis
    (B) Information Distribution System
    (C) Communication Requirements
    (D) Communications Management Plan

20. All the following would be good reasons to cancel a meeting except…

    (A) A key team member had to attend a different meeting.
    (B) The topic partially changed and the presentation material wasn't complete yet.
    (C) A Functional Manager wanted to meet with the Project Manager at the same time.
    (D) The agenda wasn't published until right before the meeting.

21. Which of the following would a Project Manager use to track stakeholder needs and open items on a project?

    (A) Change control process
    (B) Issue log
    (C) Perform integrated change control
    (D) Project management plan

22. What type of report would the Project Manager use to show what is expected to be complete in the next month on the project?

    (A) Earned Value Report
    (B) Status Report
    (C) Forecast Report
    (D) Progress Report

23. The project is approximately 70% complete and in the middle of execution. The Project Manager is communicating with Stakeholders regarding the status of the project. Which is he likely to use to ensure proper communication is delivered?

    (A) Communications Management Plan
    (B) Information Retrieval Systems
    (C) Verbal communication
    (D) Formal communication

24. The dotcom project is being stopped because the venture capitalist has stopped funding for the company. Which is the best form of communication for the management to use to communicate this information to the team members?

    (A) Verbal
    (B) Email
    (C) Formal written
    (D) Informal written

25. The Project Manager has four people reporting to him. Three more people are added to the project. How many communication channels were added to the project?

    (A) 8 channels
    (B) 10 channels
    (C) 18 channels
    (D) 20 channels

26. The wireless security system project is having problems with people not knowing about meetings and not involved in approval of project deliverables. The project is in the process of being audited by the PMO. What document would likely show information that could fix this problem?

    (A) Project management plan
    (B) Communications Management Plan
    (C) Information Distribution System
    (D) Performance Reporting Plan

27. You are the Project Manager on a medical project. You have been analyzing project data from the last six reporting periods. The main data you have been looking at is the earned value, actual cost and planned value. Which of the following will represent this data graphically?

    (A) Bar chart
    (B) S curve
    (C) Pareto diagram
    (D) Scatter diagram

28. The Project Manager is in the process of communicating to the team the tasks, their sequence, durations, and who is responsible for doing what work on the project. Which of the following contain this information?

    (A) Schedule
    (B) Gantt chart
    (C) Work Breakdown Structure
    (D) Responsibility Assignment Matrix

29.	The project has four people on it. Four more are added. What is the total number of communication channels added to the project?

(A) 6 channels
(B) 22 Channels
(C) 56 Channels
(D) 10 Channels

30.	In the communication model, who validates that the receiver has received and understood the message from the sender correctly?

(A) Both the sender and receiver
(B) Project Manager
(C) Receiver
(D) Sender

Communications Answer Key

1.   What type of report would the team member read to show what was completed in the last month on the project?

   Correct Answer: (A) Progress Report
   Explanation: The Progress Report shows what has been done in a certain time period on the project. The Status Report shows what has been completed to date on the project. The Earned Value Report focuses on Earned Value measurement. The Variance Report shows the difference between what is happening on the project, and what should have happened.

2.   In the user of the communications model, all the following would be considered by the Project Manager except…

   Correct Answer: (C) Language
   Explanation: The Communication Model includes the sender to deliver the message, the receiver to get the message, and the message as the information being exchanged.

3.   The Project Manager has been working with six influential stakeholders to determine their communication requirements. All the following could be expected as communication requirements on a project except…

   Correct Answer: (A) The name of the human resources manager for the company
   Explanation: Project status meeting time and location, steps to take regarding a project change request, and contact information for the members of the CCB would all be communication requirements on a project. The name of the HR manager would only be applicable if that person was on the project, which isn't always a given.

4.   You are the Project Manager on a medical project. You have been analyzing project data from the last two week reporting period. The main data you have been looking at involves the value of the work that should have been done, what was done, and what was paid for it. What type of report format are you looking at?

   Correct Answer: (A) Progress report
   Explanation: The Progress Report shows what has been done recently. The Status Report shows where the project is to date. The Variance Report shows the difference between what should have happened and did happen. The Performance Report is noise.

5.   You are the Project Manager for a global point of sale upgrade project that is utilizing an offshore development company. There have been a number of communication challenges with misinterpretation of requirements and failure to follow through with things associated with the store rollout that the Project Manager felt needed attention. What type of communication would help improve these problems?

   Correct Answer: (C) Formal Written
   Explanation: Formal Written communication is good when communicating details or long distance. Formal is a good answer but not as good as Formal Written. Both verbal answers would expose the project to problems.

6. The Project Manager is planning the project. He is meeting with project stakeholders to determine their communication needs for the project. He is finding out what type of information they need, when it is needed, and in what format. When done this will be added to the Project Management Plan. What will he create as a result of this work?

Correct Answer: (D) Communication Management Plan
Explanation: The Communication Management Plan helps define what the communication needs of the project are for the project team members and Stakeholders. The team list would tell who is on the team. The Staffing Management Plan would help define how to get people on the team, and Information Distribution Plan is noise.

7. What type of report would the Project Manager use to compare what has been completed to what was scheduled to be done?

Correct Answer: (C) Variance Report
Explanation: The Variance Report shows the difference between what is happening on the project and what should have happened. The Status Report shows what has been completed to date on the project. The Earned Value Report focuses on Earned Value measurement. The Progress Report shows what has been done in a certain time period on the project.

8. The Project Manager is reporting performance on a project to the stakeholders. She is reporting status on the scope, cost, and schedule of the project. What type of report is this?

Correct Answer: (A) Earned Value Report
Explanation: The Earned Value Report focuses on Earned Value measurement. The Status Report shows what has been completed to date on the project. The Progress Report shows what has been done in a certain time period on the project. The Variance Report shows the difference between what is happening on the project and what should have happened.

9. What type of report will the Project Manager use to see what has been completed so far on the software project?

Correct Answer: (B) Status Report
Explanation: The Status Report shows what has been completed to date on the project. The Earned Value Report focuses on Earned Value Measurement. The Progress Report shows what has been done in a certain time period on the project. The Variance Report shows the difference between what is happening on the project and what should have happened.

10. Which of the following would a Project Manager need to create a project progress report?

Correct Answer: (A) Work results
Explanation: Work results allow the Project Manager to report performance on the project. Status Reports are generally an output of this area. Status Reports can lead to Change Requests. Status Reports typically end up in the project archives.

11. The Project Manager has just created with the team a decomposition of the work of the project. This will aid in determining resource needs, how long the project should take and how much it should cost. What did they create?

Correct Answer: (D) Work Breakdown Structure
Explanation: The team is creating the Work Breakdown Structure (WBS). This will allow them to see what the work of the project is. The schedule shows sequencing and timelines as well as the work of the project. The Gantt chart shows bars indicating when the tasks happen. The Responsibility Assignment Matrix shows who is responsible for what areas on the project.

12. In the communication model, if the Project Manager is communicating to the receiver which of the following will they focus on delivering and ensuring that it can be decoded correctly?

    Correct Answer: (C) Message
    Explanation: In the communication model the sender conveys the message to the receiver. The feedback is the communication from the receiver to the sender to either clarify the message or acknowledge understanding. The medium is the format used to deliver the message. Noise is anything that distorts the message.

13. All the following could be considered mediums for communication by a project team member except...

    Correct Answer: (C) Message
    Explanation: The message is what is actually conveyed in the communication. The other three answers are formats for conveying information.

14. All the following are examples of communication infrastructure that a Project Manager could encounter on a project except...

    Correct Answer: (B) Spreadsheet applications
    Explanation: Spreadsheet applications are computer applications that are not necessarily part of a company's communication infrastructure.

15. The Charter on a project would be viewed as what type of communication?

    Correct Answer: (B) Formal Written
    Explanation: Any documentation associated with the contract or Project Management documentation would be considered Formal Written.

16. The Project Manager has a project team that can never keep a meeting on track because it always ends up off topic and running longer than anticipated with people bringing up side items and out of scope topics. Which of the following would improve the meetings?

    Correct Answer: (A) Create and publish an agenda, and establish the leader of the meeting
    Explanation: Creating and publishing an agenda, and knowing who is in charge of a meeting are two ways to have a highly organized effective meeting.

17. Which of the following does the Project Manager and team need to begin creating the Communications Management Plan?

    Correct Answer: (C) Project Scope Statement
    Explanation: The Project Scope Statement is an input to the Communication Management Plan. Stakeholder analysis is a tool for the process. The other two answers are noise.

18. The Project Manager spends a lot of time replying to email and meeting with stakeholders about the execution of the project. How much of a Project Manager's job is spent communicating?

    Correct Answer: (D) Approximately 90%
    Explanation: Approximately 90% of a Project Manager's time is spent communicating. This could be via e-mail, meetings, listening, speaking, web conference, etc.

19. The Project Manager is determining what the stakeholder communication needs of the project are. What will he have completed when he is done with this part of planning?

Correct Answer: (D) Communications Management Plan

Explanation: The Communications Management Plan is what defines the communication needs of the project. Stakeholder analysis is used to complete this plan by defining the communication requirements of the Stakeholders. Information Distribution System is noise.

20. All the following would be good reasons to cancel a meeting except…

Correct Answer: (C) A Functional Manager wanted to meet with the Project Manager at the same time.

Explanation: The Functional Manager wanting to meet with the Project Manager at the same time as an existing team meeting wouldn't be a good reason to cancel a meeting. The Project Manager should offer to schedule a meeting for a different time with the Functional Manager.

21. Which of the following would a Project Manager use to track stakeholder needs and open items on a project?

Correct Answer: (B) Issue log

Explanation: Issue logs are a good tool to track the status of Stakeholder needs and problems. The Change Control Process and Perform Integrated Change Control are used to review and approve changes. The Project Management Plan is the overall plan document for the project.

22. What type of report would the Project Manager use to show what is expected to be complete in the next month on the project?

Correct Answer: (C) Forecast Report

Explanation: The Forecast Report shows what is expected to happen on the project. The Status Report shows where the project is to date. The Earned Valued Report shows Earned Value data. The Progress Report shows what has been completed since the last reporting period.

23. The project is approximately 70% complete and in the middle of execution. The Project Manager is communicating with Stakeholders regarding the status of the project. Which is he likely to use to ensure proper communication is delivered?

Correct Answer: (A) Communications Management Plan

Explanation: The Communications Management Plan is used to help determine what the Stakeholders communication needs are. The other answers are noise.

24. The dotcom project is being stopped because the venture capitalist has stopped funding for the company. Which is the best form of communication for the management to use to communicate this information to the team members?

Correct Answer: (C) Formal written

Explanation: Formal written is the best form of communication to use for any "official" project documentation. Anything verbal or informal wouldn't be sufficient for official documentation and wouldn't integrate into the project archives. Email could be used, but would be under the format of Formal Written because of the message.

25. The Project Manager has four people reporting to him. Three more people are added to the project. How many communication channels were added to the project?

Correct Answer: (C) 18 channels
Explanation: The formula for communication channels is N*(N-1)/2.   First, calculate the number of communication channels based on the existing team 4 AND the Project Manager=5). That is 10 communication channels. Next, calculate the number of communication channels with the new people added. This is 28 communication channels. Finally, subtract the difference (28-10=18).

26. The wireless security system project is having problems with people not knowing about meetings and not involved in approval of project deliverables. The project is in the process of being audited by the PMO. What document would likely show information that could fix this problem?

Correct Answer: (B) Communications Management Plan
Explanation: The Communications Management Plan should show what meetings are planned, who should be involved in deliverables, signoff, and other communication needs of the project. This would be in the Project Management Plan. The other two answers are noise.

27. You are the Project Manager on a medical project. You have been analyzing project data from the last six reporting periods. The main data you have been looking at is the earned value, actual cost and planned value. Which of the following will represent this data graphically?

Correct Answer: (B) S curve
Explanation: The S curve will show the Actual Cost, Earned Value and Planned Value data over time, and Variance will be able to be observed rather easily. The Bar Chart, is also known as a Control Chart, and shows output over time. This is typically a quality chart. The Pareto Diagram shows defect by count. The Scatter Diagram displays (if applicable) a relationship between two variables.

28. The Project Manager is in the process of communicating to the team the tasks, their sequence, durations, and who is responsible for doing what work on the project. Which of the following contain this information?

Correct Answer: (A) Schedule
Explanation: This is the schedule. It consists of the Gantt chart and Work Breakdown Structure (WBS) among other items. The Responsibility Assignment Matrix shows who is responsible for what areas on the project.

29. The project has four people on it. Four more are added. What is the total number of communication channels added to the project?

Correct Answer: (B) 22 Channels
Explanation: To calculate this, you need to calculate the number of communication channels with four people. The formula is N*(N-1)/2.   This means that with four people, there are 6 channels of communication. Next, add the four additional people for a total of eight people and use the communication channel formula. This shows that there are 28 communication channels with eight people on the project. Subtract 28 from 6 for a difference, and the answer of 22 communication channels.

30. In the communication model, who validates that the receiver has received and understood the message from the sender correctly?

Correct Answer: (C) Receiver
Explanation: The sender is responsible for verifying that the message was received and interpreted correctly. This typically comes from feedback that is provided by the receiver.

Risk

1. With assistance from the team, the Project Manager has just determined what will be done as a result of uncertain events happening on the project as well as who will be responsible for monitoring and responding if the events do occur. Which of the following best describes what they have just completed?

   (A) Identify Risks
   (B) Plan Risk Responses
   (C) Secondary Response Planning
   (D) Qualitative Analysis

2. The CEO of your company is considering entering a global market with products that had been sold only locally. If your company enters it successfully, the reward could be quite significant. If the entry fails, the company could suffer significant negative impact. What would the CEO be considered?

   (A) Risk Seeker
   (B) Risk-Averse
   (C) To be meeting stockholder expectations
   (D) Risk-Neutral

3. The electrical project is scheduled to run until the end of the year. There is the possibility that the union collective contract will not be renewed immediately upon its expiration in the next month. If this happens, Senior Management has decided to shift job responsibilities around with the non-union personnel so they could be involved in the union roles on the project as well as their regular responsibilities. This would include replacing the union workers during key on call periods associated with the power grid. The goal would be to minimize the schedule slippage on the project as the union negotiation is not in their control. This is an example of what type of risk response?

   (A) Transfer
   (B) Avoid
   (C) Accept
   (D) Mitigate

4. The project team is performing risk analysis, evaluating a risk that has a very high probability of occurring. If it does, the company could go out of business. Which of the following will the risk likely be analyzed with?

   (A) Qualitative risk analysis
   (B) Insurable risk
   (C) Quantitative risk analysis
   (D) Pure risk

5.   The ecommerce system has been processing 50,000 transactions per hour. Today, the main application crashed, preventing the fulfillment of customer orders. The risk response didn't fix the problem. Which of the following steps would they perform first?

   (A) Determine why the Risk Response Plan failed
   (B) Fix the problem
   (C) Determine why the problem happened
   (D) Adjust the Risk Response Plan

6.   The printing company has added a new line for its laminating business. This involves new technology to laminate book covers quicker and cheaper. They are anticipating this will allow them to make a greater type of product and improve output efficiency. Because of the machine cost and the specific knowledge needed to repair it if it breaks, they have purchased a service contract for the machine from the manufacturer. Purchasing the service contract is an example of what?

   (A) ISO 9000
   (B) Conformance to quality
   (C) Business risk
   (D) Insurable risk

7.   The Project Manager and his team are in the planning phase of the reverse logistics project, identifying things that could go differently than planned. They are also trying to identify warning signs that would show that these events could occur. What is the team doing?

   (A) Conformance to quality
   (B) Problem solving
   (C) Risk analysis
   (D) Identifying risks

8.   The vice president of the marketing division has decided to take a "wait and see" approach to a new direction the solid state amplifier market appears to be headed in. He feels that waiting will minimize a great deal of the risk that could come with being a leader in the market, in case the market changes. What would the vice president be considered?

   (A) Risk-Neutral
   (B) To be meeting stockholder expectations
   (C) Risk-Averse
   (D) Risk Seeker

9. The airplane design project is scheduled to run until the end of the year. There is the possibility that the union contract will not be renewed upon its expiration in the next month. If this happens, Senior Management has decided to outsource the work offshore because it has no input to negotiations with the union and no assurance how long the strike could last. The date cannot slip on the schedule so options are limited. This is an example of what type of risk response?

    (A) Transfer
    (B) Avoid
    (C) Accept
    (D) Mitigate

10. The point of sale project has experienced a lot of issues and changes. The Cost Performance Index is presently 0.87 and the Schedule Performance Index is 0.85. Risk could have been managed better from the start of this project but management didn't view it a priority. Halfway through the execution of the Project Management Plan, the Project Manager assigned two people to do nothing but monitor for risks and work with the people who implemented the Risk Response Plans. What would be a main goal to achieve from risk monitoring and controlling?

    (A) Corrective Action
    (B) Quantitative Analysis
    (C) Overall Risk ranking for the project
    (D) Qualitative Analysis

11. Multiplying the probabilities by the impact of the opportunity involves using which of the following?

    (A) A Risk Rating Matrix
    (B) Expected Monetary Value (EMV)
    (C) Workarounds
    (D) Risk Triggers

12. The software company has been awarded a $100M US contract to build an enterprise application for the military. The company understands that there is a small company that has a product that complements theirs that the military will likely need to work with as well. The software company decides to acquire the complementary company to offer a more complete solution to the military. This is an example of what type of risk response strategy?

    (A) Share
    (B) Accept
    (C) Mitigate
    (D) Exploit

13. The construction project is scheduled to run until the end of the year. There is the possibility that the union collective bargaining agreement will not be renewed immediately upon its expiration in the next month. If this happens, the Project Manager and Senior Management have decided that the project will be cancelled because the union labor play a key part in the success of the project and any delay will cause a business opportunity to be missed. This is an example of what type of risk response?

    (A) Transfer
    (B) Mitigate
    (C) Avoid
    (D) Accept

14. The automotive redesign project is scheduled to run until the end of the year. There is the possibility that the union collective bargaining agreement will not be renewed immediately upon its expiration in the next month. If this happens, Senior Management has decided to give in to union demands because union labor plays a key part in the success of the project, and the project finish date cannot slip because of a government required date. This is an example of what type of risk response?

    (A) Mitigate
    (B) Transfer
    (C) Accept
    (D) Avoid

15. On the electric company project, the government implemented a regulatory change associated with the electricity sub-station upgrade project that required the company to spend an additional $400,000 US on the project. This type of cost and activity best relates to which of the following?

    (A) Known unknowns
    (B) Unknown unknowns
    (C) Management Reserve
    (D) Risk Management

16. The Project Manager will utilize which of the following in performing qualitative risk analysis?

    (A) A Risk Rating Matrix
    (B) Expected Monetary Value (EMV)
    (C) Workarounds
    (D) Risk Triggers

17. The printing company has added a new line for its laminating business. This involves new technology to laminate book covers quicker and cheaper. They are anticipating this will allow them to make a greater type of product and improve output efficiency. Adding this line is an example of what?

    (A) Business risk
    (B) ISO 9000
    (C) Conformance to quality
    (D) Insurable risk

18. The Department of Defense is involved in performing risk reviews as part of its overall risk strategy. Which of the following best describes Risk Reviews?

    (A) Determining what the characteristics of the risks are on the project
    (B) Determining what risks are on the project
    (C) Determining who will implement a Risk Response Plan
    (D) Determining the validity of the documented risks and looking for any new risks that could occur

19. The team implemented a Risk Response Plan when a vendor was found in default of a contract commitment. The response was to choose another vendor from the qualified supplier list. Because of the short notice, the other vendor cannot fulfill the need of the team because of previous commitments. Which best describes what happened with the different vendor?

    (A) Workaround
    (B) Secondary Risk
    (C) Risk Response Plan
    (D) Avoidance

20. The consulting company has created the Scope of Work for the project. It is in the process of creating a schedule and budget. It has added time into the schedule for the delays that always happen. It is also allocating money into the budget for more computers and software that are usually needed beyond what is initially forecast. These items are an example of what?

    (A) Unknown unknowns
    (B) Known unknowns
    (C) Risk Management
    (D) Management Reserve

21. A software company has been awarded a $100M US contract to build an enterprise application for the military. The company is relatively small, and this contract is bigger than anything it has been awarded to date. To ensure that it can effectively complete the contract and not jeopardize other work, it has partnered with another company more suited for larger scale deployments to do the work after it creates the core of the application. This is an example of what type of risk response strategy?

    (A) Exploit
    (B) Share
    (C) Mitigate
    (D) Accept

22.   Your company is evaluating two projects for consideration. Project A has a 40% probability of -$15,000 US and a 60% probability of $80,000 US. Project B has a 70% probability of $65,000 US and a 30% probability of -$15,000 US. Which of the projects would you select based on the greatest expected monetary value?

(A) Project A
(B) Project B
(C) Project A and B are of even value
(D) The expected monetary value is not high enough on either to make a selection

23.   Which of the following best describes risk that could occur in a technology company selling products worldwide?

(A) Either a negative or positive event
(B) Something that has already happened
(C) Negative events
(D) Positive events

24.   The Project Manager and the team are in the process of identifying risks on the project. They have decided to use categorization of risks to start out with, because the project is so large. Which of the following is the best example of risk categories?

(A) Initiating, Planning, Executing, Controlling, Closing
(B) Scope, Time, Cost
(C) Quality, Schedule, Budget
(D) External, Internal, Technology, Personnel

25.   The project team is in the process of analyzing what it will do on the project if certain events happen. It is looking at things that could go wrong, or better than expected in this analysis. Where will this information ultimately be stored?

(A) Risk trigger
(B) Risk list
(C) Risk response
(D) Risk register

26.   In Risk Management, the Risk Register contains a number of items. Risks and triggers are two of the items the Project Manager will reference from the risk register. When evaluating a Risk Trigger, which of the following is most accurate?

(A) A trigger is an indicator that a risk event will occur.
(B) A trigger is the same as a risk.
(C) A trigger is an indicator that a risk event has occurred.
(D) A trigger is an indicator that a risk event could occur.

27. The project team has created a graphical representation of the risks associated with the project to help it get better control of what could happen on the project. What have they created?

    (A) Risk Register
    (B) Prioritized list of quantified risks
    (C) Risk Management Plan
    (D) Risk Breakdown Structure

28. The team on the router and switch upgrade project is involved in planning the project. It is performing risk response planning and assigning risk owners. What is the main responsibility of the risk owner?

    (A) Watching for additional risks on the project
    (B) Watching for risk triggers and telling the Project Manager if they happen
    (C) Letting the Project Manager know that the risk has happened
    (D) Implementing a Risk Response Plan if the risk event occurs

29. Calculate the following: 0.4 probability of $5000 US, 0.3 probability of -$3500 US, 0.2 probability of $6000 US, 0.1 probability of $4000 US:

    (A) $2,700 US
    (B) $10,500 US
    (C) $2,500 US
    (D) $2,550 US

30. The software testing team is involved in developing responses to the identified risks. It could potentially create all the following except…

    (A) Residual Risks
    (B) Secondary Risk
    (C) Updates to the risk register
    (D) Risk Management Plan

Risk Answer Key

1.   With assistance from the team, the Project Manager has just determined what will be done as a result of uncertain events happening on the project as well as who will be responsible for monitoring and responding if the events do occur. Which of the following best describes what they have just completed?

   Correct Answer: (B) Plan Risk Responses
   Explanation: Plan Risk Responses documents who should do what if risk events occur. Identify Risks is the process of figuring out what risks and triggers could occur on the project. Qualitative analysis involves assigning probability and impact ratings to the risk. Secondary response planning is noise.

2.   The CEO of your company is considering entering a global market with products that had been sold only locally. If your company enters it successfully, the reward could be quite significant. If the entry fails, the company could suffer significant negative impact. What would the CEO be considered?

   Correct Answer: (A) Risk Seeker
   Explanation: A Risk Seeker mentality is that of looking for the big reward and being prepared to pay significantly if it is missed. The risk averse mentality is a very conservative approach to risk. A risk neutral mentality is somewhere between that of a Risk Seeker and risk averse mentality. The other answer is noise.

3.   The electrical project is scheduled to run until the end of the year. There is the possibility that the union collective contract will not be renewed immediately upon its expiration in the next month. If this happens, Senior Management has decided to shift job responsibilities around with the non-union personnel so they could be involved in the union roles on the project as well as their regular responsibilities. This would include replacing the union workers during key on call periods associated with the power grid. The goal would be to minimize the schedule slippage on the project as the union negotiation is not in their control. This is an example of what type of risk response?

   Correct Answer: (D) Mitigate
   Explanation: Risk mitigation is done to attempt to minimize the negative impact of the risk. In this case, management is attempting to minimize the impact of a labor strike. Risk acceptance involves simply dealing with the risk if it happens. Risk avoidance involves doing what can be done to eliminate the risk. Transference is done to assign or transfer the risk to some external party.

4.   The project team is performing risk analysis, evaluating a risk that has a very high probability of occurring. If it does, the company could go out of business. Which of the following will the risk likely be analyzed with?

   Correct Answer: (C) Quantitative risk analysis
   Explanation: Qualitative risk analysis helps determine the probability and impact of a risk. This allows the PM to have an understanding of the likelihood and the consequences of the risk. If the risk has a high probability and impact of occurring, the risk will likely go through quantitative risk analysis as well. Insurable and pure risk wouldn't fit the question here.

5. The ecommerce system has been processing 50,000 transactions per hour. Today, the main application crashed, preventing the fulfillment of customer orders. The risk response didn't fix the problem. Which of the following steps would they perform first?

    Correct Answer: (B) Fix the problem

    Explanation: This is a chicken and egg question in that you more than likely will do all the answers, but what comes first? Fixing the problem, then determining why the Risk Response Plan failed, and why the problem happened, then adjusting the Risk Response Plan would be the sequence for the other answers.

6. The printing company has added a new line for its laminating business. This involves new technology to laminate book covers quicker and cheaper. They are anticipating this will allow them to make a greater type of product and improve output efficiency. Because of the machine cost and the specific knowledge needed to repair it if it breaks, they have purchased a service contract for the machine from the manufacturer. Purchasing the service contract is an example of what?

    Correct Answer: (D) Insurable risk

    Explanation: Insurable risk is risk that you can buy insurance for, which in this case is an insurance policy that ensures what the company will have to pay if the machine breaks. Business Risk comes from simply operating the business. There is no guarantee that an idea will work as you hope. Conformance to quality relates to a proactive approach to quality. ISO9000 is a quality standard.

7. The Project Manager and his team are in the planning phase of the reverse logistics project, identifying things that could go differently than planned. They are also trying to identify warning signs that would show that these events could occur. What is the team doing?

    Correct Answer: (D) Identifying risks

    Explanation: Identifying risks should produce a list of risks and triggers. Risks are positive or negative events that can occur in the future. Triggers are indicators that a risk event could happen but is not imminent. The other three answers are noise.

8. The Vice President of the marketing division has decided to take a "wait and see" approach to a new direction the solid state amplifier market appears to be headed in. He feels that waiting will minimize a great deal of the risk that could come with being a leader in the market, in case the market changes. What would the vice president be considered?

    Correct Answer: (C) Risk-Averse

    Explanation: The Risk-Averse mentality is a very conservative approach to risk. A Risk Seeker mentality is that of looking for the big reward and being prepared to pay significantly if they miss it. A Risk-Neutral mentality is somewhere between that of a Risk Seeker and Risk-Averse mentality. The other answer is noise.

9. The airplane design project is scheduled to run until the end of the year. There is the possibility that the union contract will not be renewed upon its expiration in the next month. If this happens, Senior Management has decided to outsource the work offshore because it has no input to negotiations with the union and no assurance how long the strike could last. The date cannot slip on the schedule so options are limited. This is an example of what type of risk response?

    Correct Answer: (A) Transfer

    Explanation: Risk transference is done to assign or transfer the risk to someone else. In this case, outsourcing the work is to transfer the risk associated with labor. Risk acceptance involves simply dealing with the risk if it happens. Risk avoidance involves doing what can be done to eliminate the risk. Mitigation is done to attempt to minimize the bad risk.

10. The point of sale project has experienced a lot of issues and changes. The Cost Performance Index is presently 0.87 and the Schedule Performance Index is 0.85. Risk could have been managed better but management didn't view it as a priority initially. Halfway through the execution of the Project Management Plan, the Project Manager assigned two people to do nothing but monitor for risks and work with the people who implemented the Risk Response Plans. What would be a main goal to achieve from risk monitoring and controlling?

Correct Answer: (A) Corrective Action
Explanation: Risk monitoring and controlling involves watching for risks and implementing Risk Response Plans if the risk occurs. Qualitative and Quantitative analysis would occur before Perform Risk Responses. The overall risk ranking for the project would come from the Qualitative and Quantitative analysis.

11. Multiplying the probabilities by the impact of the opportunity involves using which of the following?

Correct Answer: (B) Expected Monetary Value (EMV)
Explanation: Expected monetary value (EMV) is used in quantitative risk analysis. This involves multiplying the probabilities by the impacts of the opportunity. This can help in generating time and cost targets for the project. Qualitative risk analysis uses a risk rating matrix to rank risks and create an overall risk rating for the project. Workarounds are done when risk events don't work. Risk triggers are indicators that a risk event could happen.

12. The software company has been awarded a $100M US contract to build an enterprise application for the military. The company understands that there is a small company that has a product that complements theirs and decides to acquire the complementary company to offer a more complete solution. This is an example of what type of risk response strategy?

Correct Answer: (D) Exploit
Explanation: Exploiting the risk is to do things to grow or expand the positive aspects of the risk. Sharing the risk is to work with someone else to maximize the risk. Mitigate would attempt to minimize the bad impact of the risk. Accepting the risk would be to tolerate whatever happened.

13. The construction project is scheduled to run until the end of the year. There is the possibility that the union collective bargaining agreement will not be renewed immediately upon its expiration in the next month. If this happens, the Project Manager and Senior Management have decided that the project will be cancelled because the union labor play a key part in the success of the project and any delay will cause a business opportunity to be missed. This is an example of what type of risk response?

Correct Answer: (D) Accept
Explanation: Risk acceptance involves simply dealing with the risk if it happens. In this case, the project would be put on hold as a means to deal with the union issue. Risk avoidance involves doing what can be done to eliminate the risk. Mitigation is done to attempt to minimize the bad risk. Transference is done to assign or transfer the risk to someone else.

14. The automotive redesign project is scheduled to run until the end of the year. There is the possibility that the union collective bargaining agreement will not be renewed immediately upon its expiration in the next month. If this happens, Senior Management has decided to give in to union demands because union labor plays a key part in the success of the project, and the project finish date cannot slip because of a government required date. This is an example of what type of risk response?

Correct Answer: (D) Avoid
Explanation: Risk avoidance involves doing what can be done to eliminate the risk. In this case, negotiating quickly for a resolution would avoid the risk. Risk acceptance involves simply dealing with the risk if it happens. Mitigation is done to attempt to minimize the bad risk. Transference is done to assign or transfer the risk to someone else.

15. On the electric company project, the government implemented a regulatory change associated with the electricity sub-station upgrade project that required the company to spend an additional $400,000 US on the project. This type of cost and activity best relates to which of the following?

Correct Answer: (B) Unknown unknowns

Explanation: Management Reserves are created for unknown unknowns. These are things that wouldn't be expected to happen. Contingency Reserves are created for known unknowns. These are things that we know will happen, we just don't know how much of it will happen. Risk Management is noise.

16. The Project Manager will utilize which of the following in performing qualitative risk analysis?

Correct Answer: (A) A Risk Rating Matrix

Explanation: Qualitative risk analysis uses a Risk Rating Matrix to rank risks and create an overall risk rating for the project. Expected Monetary Value (EMV) is used in quantitative risk analysis. Workarounds are what are done when risk events don't work. Risk triggers are indicators that a risk event could happen.

17. The printing company has added a new line for its laminating business. This involves new technology to laminate book covers quicker and cheaper. They are anticipating this will allow them to make a greater type of product and improve output efficiency. Adding this line is an example of what?

Correct Answer: (A) Business risk

Explanation: Business Risk comes from simply operating the business. There is no guarantee that an idea will work as you hope. Pure risk is also known as insurable risk. Pure Risk is a risk that you can buy insurance for. Conformance to quality is involved with quality management. ISO9000 is a quality standard.

18. The Department of Defense is involved in performing risk reviews as part of its overall risk strategy. Which of the following best describes Risk Reviews?

Correct Answer: (D) Determining the validity of the documented risks and looking for any new risks that could occur

Explanation: Risk Reviews verify that the risks are still valid and that no new risks have appeared on the project. The other three answers come before or after Risk Reviews.

19. The team implemented a Risk Response Plan when a vendor was found in default of a contract commitment. The response was to choose another vendor from the qualified supplier list. Because of the short notice, the other vendor cannot fulfill the need of the team because of previous commitments. Which best describes what happened with the different vendor?

Correct Answer: (B) Secondary Risk

Explanation: Secondary Risk is what happens when a risk event happens and creates new risk. The workaround is what is done when risk responses do not work as planned. The Risk Response Plan is to define what the risk responses will be if the risk events occur. Avoidance is a risk response strategy.

20. The consulting company has created the Scope of Work for the project. It is in the process of creating a schedule and budget. It has added time into the schedule for the delays that always happen. It is also allocating money into the budget for more computers and software that are usually needed beyond what is initially forecast. These items are an example of what?

Correct Answer: (B) Known unknowns
Explanation: Contingency Reserves are created for known unknowns. These are things that we know will happen, we just don't know how much of it will happen. Management Reserves are created for unknown unknowns. These are things that wouldn't be expected to happen. Risk Management is noise.

21. A software company has been awarded a $100M US contract to build an enterprise application for the military. The company is relatively small, and this contract is bigger than anything it has been awarded to date. To ensure that it can effectively complete the contract and not jeopardize other work, it has partnered with another company more suited for larger scale deployments to do the work after it creates the core of the application. This is an example of what type of risk response strategy?

Correct Answer: (B) Share
Explanation: Sharing the risk with another company is what is happening here. Exploiting the risk is to do things to grow or expand the positive aspects of the risk. Mitigate would attempt to minimize the bad of the risk. Accepting the risk would be to tolerate whatever happened.

22. Your company is evaluating two projects for consideration. Project A has a 40% probability of -$15,000 US and a 60% probability of $80,000 US. Project B has a 70% probability of $65,000 US and a 30% probability of -$15,000 US. Which of the projects would you select based on the greatest expected monetary value?

Correct Answer: (A) Project A
Explanation: To calculate the expected monetary value (EMV) of this question, multiply the probabilities by their dollar amount and add the product of the multiplication for each project. This results in a value of $42,000 US for Project A and $41,000 US for Project B. Project A would be selected with the highest expected monetary value (EMV).

23. Which of the following best describes risk that could occur in a technology company selling products worldwide?

Correct Answer: (A) Either a negative or positive event
Explanation: Risk can be of negative or positive consequence on a project. It is something that can happen but hasn't yet. Risk involves uncertainty that is why it involves what could happen, not what has happened.

24. The Project Manager and the team are in the process of identifying risks on the project. They have decided to use categorization of risks to start out with, because the project is so large. Which of the following is the best example of risk categories?

Correct Answer: (D) External, Internal, Technology, Personnel
Explanation: Categorization of risk means to group risks together by defining categories that they can fit into. The correct answer fits this description. The other answers are noise as they relate to the Project Management process groups or interpretations of the Triple Constraint.

25. The project team is in the process of analyzing what it will do on the project if certain events happen. It is looking at things that could go wrong, or better than expected in this analysis. Where will this information ultimately be stored?

Correct Answer: (D) Risk register
Explanation: Risk responses would end up in the Risk Register after they are created in Plan Risk Responses.

26. In Risk Management, the Risk Register contains a number of items. Risks and triggers are two of the items the Project Manager will reference from the risk register. When evaluating a Risk Trigger, which of the following is most accurate?

    Correct Answer: (D) A trigger is an indicator that a risk event could occur.
    Explanation: A trigger is something that happens that implies that a risk event might happen. Just because a trigger occurs, it doesn't automatically assume that a risk will happen.

27. The project team has created a graphical representation of the risks associated with the project to help it get better control of what could happen on the project. What have they created?

    Correct Answer: (D) Risk Breakdown Structure
    Explanation: The Risk Breakdown Structure (RBS) is a graphical representation of the risk categorization and risks within those categories of the project. The risk management plan is the management approach to risk on the project. The Risk Register contains Risk Lists, analysis, responses and risk owners for the project. Prioritized list of quantified risks would come in the risk register and involves risk ranking, not identification categorization.

28. The team on the router and switch upgrade project is involved in planning the project. It is performing risk response planning and assigning risk owners. What is the main responsibility of the risk owner?

    Correct Answer: (D) Implementing a risk response plan if the risk event occurs
    Explanation: Risk owners are responsible for implementing a risk response plan that is assigned to them. Watching for additional risks on the project could fall under the responsibility of a Risk Owner, but it wouldn't be the main responsibility. Letting the Project Manager know that a risk event has happened wouldn't be the main responsibility of the risk owner. Watching for risk triggers and telling the Project Manager if they happen isn't taking a proactive approach to risk or Project Management.

29. Calculate the following: 0.4 probability of $5000 US, 0.3 probability of -$3500 US, 0.2 probability of $6000 US, 0.1 probability of $4000 US:

    Correct Answer: (D) $2,550 US
    Explanation: To calculate the expected monetary value (EMV) of this question, multiply each probability by its dollar amount and add the multiplication products. This results in a value of $2550.

30. The software testing team is involved in developing responses to the identified risks. It could potentially create all the following except...

    Correct Answer: (D) Risk Management Plan
    Explanation: The Risk Management Plan is created in Plan Risk Management. Of the remaining answers, not all will be created in Plan Risk Responses but can be created if certain events happen.

Procurement

1. The project team is involved in a make-or-buy analysis. The members have decided it is best to buy the products needed instead of creating the products internally. They are evaluating the contract format to use to minimize their risk. This will likely mean shifting the risk to the seller. What type of contract will provide the seller with the most risk when entering into a contract?

    (A) Cost Plus Percentage Cost
    (B) Fixed Price
    (C) Time and Materials
    (D) Purchase Order

2. Your company is involved in an integrated circuit project in which the information and intellectual property associated with it are highly sensitive resulting in the only product in this market. The project will involve people from a variety of skill sets on the project. Given this, which of the following would make the most sense when planning the project?

    (A) Outsourcing to an offshore development facility so your local competitors won't know your intellectual property details
    (B) The company making the product internally
    (C) The company outsourcing and having the partner sign a non-disclosure agreement
    (D) Having only the creators of the idea work on the project to control who knows about the intellectual property

3. Your company is working with a staffing company for supplementing an Internet developer for your newest project. The cost is $80 US per hour. The developer will work on the project until it is complete, then the contract will end. What type of contract is this?

    (A) Cost Plus Incentive Fee
    (B) Fixed Price
    (C) Time and Materials
    (D) Cost Plus

4. The retail chain is using a vendor to provide engineers for a security camera network design and implementation. Presently, the team is negotiating a contract that will help select the vendor. They are negotiating criteria that will reward the engineers for network performance. This is a new type of approach the company is utilizing. What best described this type of criteria?

    (A) Standard Terms
    (B) Special Provisions
    (C) Detailed Negotiations
    (D) Standard Conditions

5. You are in the process of purchasing 125 bed frames, mattresses, dressers and televisions for an upcoming project to remodel a hotel. What type of contract will you likely use?

   (A) Purchase Order
   (B) Fixed Price
   (C) Cost Plus Percentage Cost
   (D) Net 30

6. An airport is buying services from a construction company to put in a new runway for $40M US over four years. At the start of each year, the amount fluctuates relative to the national cost of living. This is an example of what type of contract?

   (A) Cost Plus
   (B) Fixed Price Incentive Fee
   (C) Fixed Price Economic Price Adjust
   (D) Fixed Price

7. The construction project is beginning the initial stages of procurement. The Project Manager is evaluating the best type of contract for the work. He decides to not use the cost plus percentage of cost as the buyer has said they want no part of that type of contract. Why is a cost plus percentage cost contract bad for the buyer?

   (A) It provides no reason for the buyer to control the costs.
   (B) It requires use of a more detailed Request for Proposal (RFP).
   (C) It requires the seller to audit all costs incurred.
   (D) It provides no reason for the seller to control costs.

8. Your company just completed a make-or-buy decision regarding a new product line to complement a service your company offers. The company has decided to buy the product line and resell it under their own branding. As a result of this decision, it is concerned about risk exposure in the contract type. Which type of contract would it prefer to use if it wants to control costs and minimize risk?

   (A) Purchase Order
   (B) Unilateral Order
   (C) Cost Plus Percentage of Costs
   (D) Fixed Price

9. The retail chain is using a vendor to provide engineers for a security camera network design and implementation. Presently, the team is negotiating a contract with potential vendors. What is the main goal of negotiations?

   (A) To attain the best price possible for the seller
   (B) To attain the best price possible for the buyer
   (C) To attain a fair price for the buyer and seller
   (D) To attain a fair price for the seller to get more work from the buyer

Procurement

10. The contract is expected to cost $280K US. Actual costs are $240K US. There is a 50/50% share for any cost savings. What is the total value of the contract?

    (A) $240K US
    (B) $260K US
    (C) $300K US
    (D) $280K US

11. The procurement process at your company is normally extremely complicated and time-consuming. A new initiative is put in place to use a qualified sellers list to help make the process more efficient. All the following are advantages of using a qualified sellers list except...

    (A) Provides a list of pre-qualified vendors
    (B) Provides the ability to work with vendors that are compatible with your company's processes
    (C) Provides contracts without negotiations
    (D) Provides a list of vendors that meet your industry standards

12. In considering a make-or-buy analysis with business goals, your company has all the following are reasons for outsourcing work except...

    (A) Your company doesn't possess the skills needed for the work
    (B) Your company doesn't have excess capacity for the work
    (C) Your company isn't concerned about protecting the information associated with the work
    (D) Your company has excess capacity for the work

13. The retail chain is using a vendor to provide engineers for a security camera network design and implementation. Presently, the team is involved in negotiating a contract that will result in selection of a vendor to perform the work under the contract. In what process is the team involved?

    (A) Conduct Procurements
    (B) Administer Procurements
    (C) Plan Procurements
    (D) Close Procurements

14. The retail chain is using a vendor to provide engineers for a security camera network design and implementation. The team has been completing the work they agreed upon. Both parties are communicating via status reports. The seller has submitted the first payment request. In what process is the team involved?

    (A) Plan Procurements
    (B) Conduct Procurements
    (C) Administer Procurements
    (D) Close Procurements

15. In evaluating contracts, there are a number of components that make a contract enforceable. All the following items are needed to make a contract legal except...

    (A) An offer
    (B) Legal purpose
    (C) Negotiation
    (D) Consideration

16. The retail chain is using a vendor to provide engineers for a security camera network design and implementation. Presently, the team is meeting with potential vendors, showing them the details of the work of the project they would be involved in, as well as answering any questions they have about the work before their proposals are submitted. What is this called?

    (A) Select Sellers
    (B) Request for Information
    (C) Conduct Procurements
    (D) Bidders Conference

17. All the following would be considered benefits of a centralized contracting environment except...

    (A) Career path for Contract Administrators
    (B) Expertise in the contracting area
    (C) Contract Administrators have teammates for contract related support
    (D) Lack of career path for Contract Administrators

18. The retail chain is using a vendor to provide engineers for a security camera network design and implementation. Presently, the seller is having issues getting paid from the retailer and chooses to inform the buyer that they are in default of the contract. The seller then decides to remove the engineers from the job site, effectively stopping all project work since they haven't been paid by the buyer yet. What most accurately describes this situation?

    (A) The buyer is wrong in stopping payment until the issue is resolved.
    (B) The buyer is right in stopping payment until the issue is resolved.
    (C) The seller is wrong and needs to correct the situation.
    (D) Both sides appear to be in default of the contract.

19. The retail chain is using a vendor to provide engineers for a security camera network design and implementation. The buyer of the solution is providing requirements that the solution needs to be able to accomplish when the solution is complete. What type of Scope of Work is being utilized on this project?

    (A) Functionality
    (B) Design
    (C) Analogous
    (D) Cost Plus

20. You are the owner of a house painting company. You occasionally have the need for an automated paint sprayer. This tool sells for $2000 US and would cost $20 a day to maintain. You can rent one for $175 a day with maintenance included. How many days would you need to use this tool before it would make sense to buy the tool instead of rent?

    (A) Six days
    (B) Twelve days
    (C) Eight days
    (D) Thirteen days

21. The company typically spends a large amount of time dealing with procurement issues. A lot of this involves creation of procurement documents and bidders conferences. The company has recently considered shifting to non-competitive forms of procurement where it makes business sense to do so. Which of the following would they use for this?

    (A) Single source
    (B) Qualified Sellers List
    (C) Evaluation criteria
    (D) Screening system

22. A single-phase construction project is in the process of closing. There are a number of processes coming together as things finish up to complete the work of the project. Which of the following is correct?

    (A) Close Project or Phase happens only if the project is completed as planned
    (B) Close Project or Phase will come before Close Procurements
    (C) Close Project or Phase and Close Procurements happen at the same time
    (D) Close Procurements will come before Close Project or Phase

23. The retail chain is using a vendor to provide engineers for a security camera network design and implementation. The team has received six proposals from companies interested in doing the work. In what process is the team involved?

    (A) Plan Procurements
    (B) Conduct Procurements
    (C) Select Sellers
    (D) Plan Contracting

24. The retail chain is using a vendor to provide engineers for a security camera network design and implementation. The sellers are receiving a very detailed description of the work that is anticipated to be involved in the project. What type of Scope of Work is being provided to the sellers?

    (A) Functionality
    (B) Design
    (C) Analogous
    (D) Cost Plus

25. The retail chain will be using a vendor to provide engineers for a security camera network design and implementation. The team is determining the details needed for the documentation that will help select the company to provide the services. This also includes evaluation criteria for comparing the proposals received. In what process is the team involved?

    (A) Plan Contracting
    (B) Plan Procurements
    (C) Select Sellers
    (D) Conduct Procurements

26. The retail chain is using a vendor to provide engineers for a security camera network design and implementation. The equipment buyer is providing the list of models and quantity of each piece of equipment to be purchased plus the purchase timeframes. What type of document is being provided to the sellers?

    (A) Invitation for Bid (IFB)
    (B) Request for Information (RFI)
    (C) Request for Proposals (RFP)
    (D) Request for Quote (RFQ)

27. Two contract officers are discussing the best type of contract to use for purchasing commodity type items. One person is saying a fixed price contract is the best, and the other person is saying a unilateral contract is best. Which of the following best describes a unilateral contract?

    (A) The buyer and seller establish contract parameters during a single negotiation session.
    (B) The seller establishes a not to exceed price for the buyer to accept or reject.
    (C) The buyer establishes a not to exceed price for the seller to accept or reject.
    (D) The seller establishes a price, and the buyer simply has to purchase the item.

28. The retail chain is using a vendor to provide engineers for a security camera network design and implementation. The sellers received a detailed description of what the buyer wants, including details associated with a request for a customized solution. What type of document is being provided to the sellers?

    (A) Request for Proposal (RFP)
    (B) Request for Information (RFI)
    (C) Request for Quote (RFQ)
    (D) Invitation for Bid (IFB)

29. You are the Project Manager working with the customer on a data warehouse development project. Your company is responsible for the internal personnel and their hours of effort. The customer needs some modifications to the Scope of the project due to some new functionality being available that wasn't available when the project started. This modification will require the Scope of Work to the contract to be modified. Who can modify the contract?

    (A) Contract Administrator
    (B) The Project Manager for the buyer
    (C) The Project Manager for the seller
    (D) The Project Manager for the buyer and seller

30. You've hired a company to produce a course curriculum but aren't sure of the detail needed. It agrees to pay the supplier for costs and a fee of $5.6K US. What type of contract is this?

    (A) Time and Materials
    (B) Fixed Price
    (C) Cost Plus
    (D) Cost Plus Fixed Fee

Procurement Answer Key

1. The project team is involved in a make-or-buy analysis. The members have decided it is best to buy the products needed instead of creating the products internally. They are evaluating the contract format to use to minimize their risk. This will likely mean shifting the risk to the seller. What type of contract will provide the seller with the most risk when entering into a contract?

    Correct Answer: (B) Fixed Price
    Explanation: The Fixed Price contract provides the seller with the most risk because the contract limits the amount that the buyer will pay for the project, meaning that the seller needs to have a detailed understanding of exactly what is needed on the project so it can control costs. Cost Plus Percentage of Cost provides the least risk to the seller. A purchase order provides the seller with no risk because the price for a commodity type item has been established. Time and materials contracts are typically used for smaller amounts of work and staff augmentation.

2. Your company is involved in an integrated circuit project in which the information and intellectual property associated with it are highly sensitive resulting in the only product in this market. The project will involve people from a variety of skill sets on the project. Given this, which of the following would make the most sense when planning the project?

    Correct Answer: (B) The company making the product internally
    Explanation: When intellectual property and proprietary information are involved, it makes sense for a company to keep the work internal. Having an outsourcing partner sign a non-disclosure agreement is not the best answer. The other two answers are noise.

3. Your company is working with a staffing company for supplementing an Internet developer for your newest project. The cost is $80 US per hour. The developer will work on the project until it is complete, then the contract will end. What type of contract is this?

    Correct Answer: (C) Time and Materials
    Explanation: A Time and Materials contract (T&M) is typically used for smaller projects or staff augmentation, such as this example. The Fixed Price contract has a seller doing work for a set price. The Cost Plus contract pays a seller costs plus a negotiated fee. The Cost Plus Incentive Fee pays a seller costs plus an incentive fee for meeting performance goals.

4. The retail chain is using a vendor to provide engineers for a security camera network design and implementation. Presently, the team is negotiating a contract that will help select the vendor. It is negotiating criteria that will reward the engineers for network performance. This is a new type of approach the company is utilizing. What best described this type of criteria?

    Correct Answer: (B) Special Provisions
    Explanation: Special Provisions are extra items that are added to a contract after negotiations have occurred. Standard Terms and Conditions are typically part of a template the company will use in a contract. Detailed negotiation is noise.

5. You are in the process of purchasing 125 bed frames, mattresses, dressers and televisions for an upcoming project to remodel a hotel. What type of contract will you likely use?

    Correct Answer: (A) Purchase Order
    Explanation: The Purchase Order is a general purchase vehicle for commodity type purchases. It is typically for items that are standard, non-customized and non-negotiable in price. Fixed price is typically for a detailed, customized, negotiated solution. Cost Plus Percentage of Cost is an outdated contract type, and not good for the buyer. Net 30 is noise.

6. An airport is buying services from a construction company to put in a new runway for $40M US over four years. At the start of each year, the amount fluctuates relative to the national cost of living. This is an example of what type of contract?

    Correct Answer: (C) Fixed Price Economic Price Adjust
    Explanation: A Fixed Price Economic Price Adjust contract deals with offering a contract that generally has a fixed price, but because of contract length, will adjust year by year as a neutral economic indicator moves upward or downward. The Fixed Price contract has a seller doing work for a set price. The Cost Plus contract pays a seller costs plus a negotiated fee. The Fixed Price Incentive Fee pays a seller a fixed price plus an incentive fee for meeting performance goals.

7. The construction project is beginning the initial stages of procurement. The Project Manager is evaluating the best type of contract for the work. He decides to not use the cost plus percentage of cost as the buyer has said they want no part of that type of contract. Why is a cost plus percentage cost contract bad for the buyer?

    Correct Answer: (D) It provides no reason for the seller to control costs.
    Explanation: In a Cost Plus Percentage of Cost contract, the seller is paid a fee that is a percentage of the total cost. As a result of this characteristic of the contract, there is no incentive for the seller to control the costs. The other three answers are noise.

8. Your company just completed a make-or-buy decision regarding a new product line to complement a service your company offers. The company has decided to buy the product line and resell it under their own branding. As a result of this decision, it is concerned about risk exposure in the contract type. Which type of contract would it prefer to use if it wants to control costs and minimize risk?

    Correct Answer: (D) Fixed Price
    Explanation: The Fixed Price contract puts a maximum on costs and should provide the minimum risk exposure to the buyer because the maximum risk is absorbed by the seller. Cost Plus Percentage of Costs has a great risk and no cost control for the buyer. Purchase Orders are typically used to purchase commodity type items. Unilateral Order is noise in this question.

9. The retail chain is using a vendor to provide engineers for a security camera network design and implementation. Presently, the team is negotiating a contract with potential vendors. What is the main goal of negotiations?

    Correct Answer: (C) To attain a fair price for the buyer and seller
    Explanation: The main goal of negotiations is to attain a fair price for the buyer and seller. This will help foster a long-term relationship. Attaining the best price possible for one side and not the other creates a win/lose relationship. Attaining a fair price to attain future work isn't an ideal approach because there is no guarantee that the future work will be there.

10. The contract is expected to cost $280K US. Actual costs are $240K US. There is a 50/50% share for any cost savings. What is the total value of the contract?

   Correct Answer: (B) $260K US
   Explanation: This is a calculation question. The $280K US is the expected value of the contract. Actual cost of the contract is $240K US. This means that there is $40K US saved. The 50/50% Share means that $20K US of the savings would go to the seller. The Actual Cost of $240K US and $20K US saving Share makes the total value of the contract worth $260K US.

11. The procurement process at your company is normally extremely complicated and time-consuming. A new initiative is put in place to use a qualified sellers list to help make the process more efficient. All the following are advantages of using a qualified sellers list except...

   Correct Answer: (C) Provides contracts without negotiations
   Explanation: A Qualified Sellers List doesn't provide contracts without negotiations. All contracts can include negotiations. The other three answers are advantages of using a qualified sellers list.

12. In considering a make-or-buy analysis with business goals, your company has all the following are reasons for outsourcing work except...

   Correct Answer: (D) Your company has excess capacity for the work
   Explanation: An excess capacity to do work is a good reason not to outsource the work. The other answers are good reasons to outsource the work.

13. The retail chain is using a vendor to provide engineers for a security camera network design and implementation. Presently, the team is involved in negotiating a contract that will result in selection of a vendor to perform the work under the contract. In what process is the team involved?

   Correct Answer: (A) Conduct Procurements
   Explanation: Conduct Procurements involves receiving and reviewing proposals from companies being considered for the work. Administer Procurements involves management of the contract itself. Plan Procurements analyzes procurement or outsourcing needs. Close Procurements validates that the contract terms and conditions have been met.

14. The retail chain is using a vendor to provide engineers for a security camera network design and implementation. The team has been completing the work they agreed upon. Both parties are communicating via status reports. The seller has submitted the first payment request. In what process is the team involved?

   Correct Answer: (C) Administer Procurements
   Explanation: Administer Procurements involves management of the contract itself. Plan Procurements analyzes procurement or outsourcing needs. Conduct Procurements involves receiving and reviewing proposals from companies being considered for the work. Close Procurements validates that the contract terms and conditions have been met.

15. In evaluating contracts, there are a number of components that make a contract enforceable. All the following items are needed to make a contract legal except...

   Correct Answer: (C) Negotiation
   Explanation: Negotiation is not needed to make a contract legal. If the buyer and seller are in agreement on the offer and consideration, negotiation is not required. The other answers are all required to make a contract legal. This can include Capacity, Offer, Consideration, Legal, and Acceptance.

16. The retail chain is using a vendor to provide engineers for a security camera network design and implementation. Presently, the team is meeting with potential vendors, showing them the details of the work of the project they would be involved in, as well as answering any questions they have about the work before their proposals are submitted. What is this called?

Correct Answer: (D) Bidders Conference
Explanation: A Bidders Conference is used to allow companies that are considering bidding on a project to learn more about the work of the project and ask any questions. The questions and answers are made available to all considering bidding for the work. Conduct Procurements is a process to find companies that can do the work. Request for Information is a procurement document. Select Sellers is noise.

17. All the following would be considered benefits of a centralized contracting environment except...

Correct Answer: (D) Lack of career path for Contract Administrators
Explanation: Centralized contracting provides a functional type of environment for the role, meaning that there is a career path for the person, instead of a lack of career path. The other answers fit the description of advantages for Centralized Contracting.

18. The retail chain is using a vendor to provide engineers for a security camera network design and implementation. Presently, the seller is having issues getting paid from the retailer and chooses to inform the buyer that they are in default of the contract. The seller then decides to remove the engineers from the job site, effectively stopping all project work since they haven't been paid by the buyer yet. What most accurately describes this situation?

Correct Answer: (D) Both sides appear to be in default of the contract.
Explanation: If the seller isn't performing as defined in the contract, it could be in default of the contract. The buyer choosing to stop payment creates a default situation as well. Two wrongs do not make a right in this case. The buyer is not right in stopping payment just because the other side is in default. The other two answers are both accurate, but they are not the best answer.

19. The retail chain is using a vendor to provide engineers for a security camera network design and implementation. The buyer of the solution is providing requirements that the solution needs to be able to accomplish when the solution is complete. What type of Scope of Work is being utilized on this project?

Correct Answer: (A) Functionality
Explanation: The functionality Scope of Work shows the general functional specifications that the outcome of the project needs to have when complete. A design Scope of Work shows specifically what is to be created. Cost Plus and analogous are noise.

20. You are the owner of a house painting company. You occasionally have the need for an automated paint sprayer. This tool sells for $2000 US and would cost $20 a day to maintain. You can rent one for $175 a day with maintenance included. How many days would you need to use this tool before it would make sense to buy the tool instead of rent?

Correct Answer: (D) Thirteen days
Explanation: To complete this question, solve for the number of days. The number of days will be the variable D in the formula. $2000+20D=$175D is the formula. First, move D to one side of the equation. Subtracting $20D from both sides gives $2000=$155D. Next, divide both sides by 155, which isolates D. That equals 12.9 (rounded), which means you would need to use the tool for thirteen full days before it would make sense to buy the tool.

21. The company typically spends a large amount of time dealing with procurement issues. A lot of this involves creation of procurement documents and bidders conferences. The company has recently considered shifting to non-competitive forms of procurement where it makes business sense to do so. Which of the following would they use for this?

   Correct Answer: (A) Single source
   Explanation: One type of non-competitive forms of procurement is single source, in which a single company is chosen even though others are available. The other form is sole source, in which there is only one source available. Generally, the provider possesses a patent or some other type of ownership associated with intellectual property. The other three answers are noise.

22. A single-phase construction project is in the process of closing. There are a number of processes coming together as things finish up to complete the work of the project. Which of the following is correct?

   Correct Answer: (D) Close Procurements will come before Close Project or Phase
   Explanation: The contract would be closed out before the Close Project or Phase process. Close project or Phase happens regardless of how the project ends.

23. The retail chain is using a vendor to provide engineers for a security camera network design and implementation. The team has received six proposals from companies interested in doing the work. In what process is the team involved?

   Correct Answer: (B) Conduct Procurements
   Explanation: Conduct Procurements involves receiving and reviewing proposals from companies being considered for the work. Plan Procurements analyzes procurement or outsourcing needs. Select Sellers and Plan Contracting are noise.

24. The retail chain is using a vendor to provide engineers for a security camera network design and implementation. The sellers are receiving a very detailed description of the work that is anticipated to be involved in the project. What type of Scope of Work is being provided to the sellers?

   Correct Answer: (B) Design
   Explanation: A design Scope of Work shows specifically what is to be created. The functionality Scope of Work shows the general functional specifications that the outcome of the project needs to have when complete. Cost Plus and Analogous are noise.

25. The retail chain will be using a vendor to provide engineers for a security camera network design and implementation. The team is determining the details needed for the documentation that will help select the company to provide the services. This also includes evaluation criteria for comparing the proposals received. In what process is the team involved?

   Correct Answer: (B) Plan Procurements
   Explanation: Plan Procurements analyzes procurement or outsourcing needs. Conduct Procurements involves receiving and reviewing proposals from companies being considered for the work. Select Sellers and Plan Contracting are noise.

26. The retail chain is using a vendor to provide engineers for a security camera network design and implementation. The equipment buyer is providing the list of models and quantity of each piece of equipment to be purchased plus the purchase timeframes. What type of document is being provided to the sellers?

Correct Answer: (D) Request for Quote (RFQ)

Explanation: A Request for Quotes (RFQ) involves getting prices from a company for goods or services. A Request for Proposal (RFP) deals with a detailed, very specific approach to a customized solution. A Request for Information (RFI) deals with finding potential vendors for consideration for proposals or quotes. An Invitation for Bid (IFB) is similar to the RFP but is typically used in government contracting.

27. Two contract officers are discussing the best type of contract to use for purchasing commodity type items. One person is saying a fixed price contract is the best, and the other person is saying a unilateral contract is best. Which of the following best describes a unilateral contract?

Correct Answer: (D) The seller establishes a price, and the buyer simply has to purchase the item.

Explanation: A Purchase Order is an example of a unilateral contract. In a unilateral contract, the seller establishes a price and the buyer has the option to purchase at that price. Thus, uni means one-sided on the negotiations. The other three answers are noise.

28. The retail chain is using a vendor to provide engineers for a security camera network design and implementation. The sellers received a detailed description of what the buyer wants, including details associated with a request for a customized solution. What type of document is being provided to the sellers?

Correct Answer: (A) Request for Proposal (RFP)

Explanation: A Request for Proposals (RFP) deals with a detailed, very specific approach to a customized solution. A Request for Information (RFI) deals with finding potential vendors for consideration for proposals or quotes. A Request for Quotes involves getting prices from a company for goods or services. An Invitation for Bid (IFB) is similar to the RFP but typically used in government contracting.

29. You are the Project Manager working with the customer on a data warehouse development project. Your company is responsible for the internal personnel and their hours of effort. The customer needs some modifications to the Scope of the project due to some new functionality being available that wasn't available when the project started. This modification will require the Scope of Work to the contract to be modified. Who can modify the contract?

Correct Answer: (A) Contract Administrator

Explanation: The Contract Administrator is the only person with the authority to change the contract. The Project Managers from the buyer and the seller will likely have input to the changes, but the Contract Administrator will be the person making those changes to the contract.

30. You've hired a company to produce a course curriculum but aren't sure of the detail needed. It agrees to pay the supplier for costs and a fee of $5.6K US. What type of contract is this?

Correct Answer: (D) Cost Plus Fixed Fee

Explanation: The Cost Plus Fixed Fee pays a seller costs plus a negotiated fixed fee. A Time and Materials contract (T&M) is typically used for smaller projects or staff augmentation. The Fixed Price contract has a seller doing work for a set price. The Cost Plus contract pays a seller a costs plus a negotiated fee.

Full CAPM® Exam Simulation

1. Project planning is ongoing as the team analyzes how long it will take to process a new order and a change order through the new call center. This analysis will help them determine how many employees to have in the call center based on their demand as anticipated by customer volume. This is an example of what?

   (A) Assumptions
   (B) Constraints
   (C) Operations management
   (D) Strategic planning

2. The Project Manager and her team are involved in establishing the costs of the project and applying it to the schedule to determine when these costs will happen on the project. Which of the following are they doing?

   (A) Determine Budget
   (B) Cost Baseline
   (C) Estimate Costs
   (D) Control Costs

3. In performing a project, the team will focus on the project life cycle and the project management life cycle. What are the five phases of a Project Management Life Cycle (PMLC)?

   (A) Initiating, Planning Executing, Testing, Closure
   (B) Requirements, System Development, Testing, UAT
   (C) Initiating, Planning Executing, Testing, Signoff
   (D) Initiating, Planning, Executing, Monitoring and Controlling, Closing

4. The Project Manager is considering quitting his job to develop a book, and supporting products for the PMP® Exam, an idea he created outside his job. If it sells well, he plans to start his own company and sell them full time. What characteristic is he showing toward risk?

   (A) Risk Seeker
   (B) Risk-Averse
   (C) To be meeting stockholder expectations
   (D) Risk Neutral

5. All the following could be considered functions of the GERT diagramming method except…

   (A) Some activities may be performed only in part.
   (B) Some activities may be fast tracked.
   (C) Some activities may be performed more than once.
   (D) Some activities may not be performed.

6. The planning is progressing on schedule for the hotel renovation project. The Project Manager and the team are ready to begin estimating costs. The customer needs an estimate as soon as possible. What estimating method should the team use?

    (A) Parametric estimating
    (B) Analogous estimating
    (C) Bottom up estimating
    (D) Estimate Costs

7. You are a Project Manager assigned to a project that has spent $4,000,000 US. The original budget was $1,500,000. Senior management is considering stopping this project. What term describes the $1,500,000 that has been spent so far?

    (A) The budgeted cost of work performed
    (B) Opportunity cost
    (C) Sunk cost
    (D) Expected Monetary Value

8. The Project Manager is having a team meeting and explaining to the team the upcoming milestones that are due. What are the characteristics of a milestone?

    (A) A duration of zero (0)
    (B) The completion of a major event in the project
    (C) The completion of major deliverables
    (D) All the above

9. A new tape backup server has just been purchased for backing up the company's development and release software. The tape backup server costs $50,000 US, and it was necessary to upgrade the local area network with an Ethernet switch at a cost of $10,000. The Project Manager is told that she needs to set up a depreciation schedule for the tape backup server over a five-year period with a value of $0 at the end of this period. She will use standard depreciation in the calculation. What is the amount per year the server will depreciate?

    (A) Not enough information
    (B) $10,000 US
    (C) $20,000 US
    (D) $14,000 US

10. You are doing quality planning on a project. The Sponsor puts into the charter that the quality standard wanted on the project is +/- 2 sigma. This translates to what percentage?

    (A) 95.46%
    (B) 68.26%
    (C) 99.73%
    (D) 50%

11. The team has just completed the process of evaluating the success of the data cleansing project. The team members analyzed how the approach to running the project worked. They evaluated the planning and executing. They documented how the Sponsor and Senior Management supported the project as well as the conflicts that were generated by three Functional Managers. What have they just completed?

    (A) Lessons Learned
    (B) Project closure
    (C) Procurement audit
    (D) Administrative closure

12. Flexibility with an activity on a Network diagram is also known as what?

    (A) GERT
    (B) PERT
    (C) Lag
    (D) Slack

13. The Project Manager is working with the customer to gain formal acceptance on the documentation deliverables for a software project. The customer is saying that the deliverables are unusable in their present form as they don't align with the project requirements. Upon reviewing documentation, the customer tells the Project Manager that the requirements are not accurate to meet the needs for which the project was undertaken. Which of the following will help fix this problem?

    (A) Creating the work breakdown structure
    (B) Control Scope
    (C) Define Scope
    (D) Verify Scope

14. A Project Manager studying different motivation theories is impressed with one theory which states that people are not motivated by money but by self actualization. To what theory is the Project Manager referring?

    (A) McGregor's Theory of X and Y
    (B) Maslow's hierarchy
    (C) Herzberg's Theory
    (D) None of the above

15. The team has had five meetings to decompose the work of the aircraft carrier project. They are making progress and in a few more meetings should have all the decomposition complete for the multi year project. All the following are benefits of using a WBS except...

    (A) Describes the deliverables of the project
    (B) Helps the project team understand their role and buy-in on the project
    (C) Provides the justification for staff, cost, and time
    (D) Identifies special work packages that can be created outside the WBS, but within the project

16. A project will be using a company to provide technicians for a distribution center project. Presently, the Project Manager is in contract negotiation with a vendor and the negotiations are going too smooth. In what process is the Project Manager involved?

    (A) Plan Procurements
    (B) Close Procurements
    (C) Conduct Procurements
    (D) Administer Procurements

17. As the buyer is involved in creating Request For Proposals (RFP) for an infrastructure project, they will provide these to sellers of services. All the following are names used for a seller except…

    (A) Service provider
    (B) Acquiring organization
    (C) Supplier
    (D) Contractor

18. Crosswind Custom Homes is building a customer's dream house. However, rain has delayed the finish by three weeks. The schedule shows that the next task is to install the windows followed by the outside siding. This is an example of what?

    (A) Mandatory dependencies
    (B) Crashing
    (C) Lag
    (D) Discretionary dependencies

19. The Project Manager and Functional Manager are having a disagreement on resource allocation for a new broadband project. The Functional Manager wants the resource for an operational issue that needs attention, and the Project Manager wants the resource to work on the project so it stays on schedule as planned. Which of the following roles can help resolve this problem?

    (A) Sponsor
    (B) Project management
    (C) Functional management
    (D) Senior management

20. The Project Manager is creating a network diagram to show the sequencing on the project. He is using a method which includes dummies. All the following Network diagram techniques display this dependency except...

    (A) Activity on Line (AOL)
    (B) Arrow Diagramming Method (ADM)
    (C) Activity on Arrow (AOA)
    (D) Activity on Node (AON)

21. The Project Manager for the hotel development project is utilizing a Responsibility Assignment Matrix (RAM) to help make project execution go easier. What will this do for the Project Manager?

    (A) Shows who is on the project
    (B) Shows who is to perform the work and how long it will take
    (C) Shows what order the tasks come in
    (D) Shows who is to perform work in certain areas of the project

22. The Project Manager has been negotiating with an integrated circuit vendor for the last six months. The vendor received the Statement of Work and has responded with a proposal using fixed fee pricing. The Project Manager answers back with a letter of intent. Why did the Project Manager send this letter?

    (A) The Project Manager plans to request a bid from the vendor.
    (B) The Project Manager plans to buy from the vendor.
    (C) The Project Manager plans to sue the vendor.
    (D) The Project Manager plans to buy the vendor.

23. The project is in a Projectized environment. There are significant challenges with meeting the tight schedule of the project and personnel leaving the company. Project personnel have been complaining to senior management about the environment hoping for a resolution. In this type of environment, who controls the resources?

    (A) Project Manager
    (B) Functional Manager
    (C) Senior Management
    (D) Project Coordinator

24. A Project Manager has completed the scope statement of the project. The customer and Sponsor have shortened the schedule by four weeks and decided that the work breakdown structure will be excluded. The Project Manager informs the customer and Sponsor that this process creates the Work Breakdown Structure (WBS) for their project. Which answer best explains why the WBS is so important to a project?

    (A) It provides templates that can be reused on other projects.
    (B) It helps in team commitment to the project.
    (C) It provides a hierarchical diagram of the project.
    (D) It is used for estimating activities, cost, and resources.

25. The team is testing the work of the project and is having issues with a particular requirement showing the desired data. Which of the following can they use to isolate the problem?

    (A) Ishikawa Diagram
    (B) Cost-Benefit Analysis
    (C) Design of Experiments
    (D) Flowcharts

26. The buyer has requested that the seller of services for a credit card processing project sign a fixed price contract. Fixed price contracts are also known as which of the following?

    (A) Lump Sum
    (B) Cost Plus
    (C) Time and Materials
    (D) Purchase Order

27. The Project Manager is creating planning documentation that will align the cost tracking with the Work Breakdown Structure (WBS) and the organizational chart. What is the Project Manager creating?

    (A) Chart of accounts
    (B) Work packages
    (C) Cost baseline
    (D) Cost estimates

28. Which of the following fits the description of the person who will pay for the work and possibly own it when it is complete?

    (A) Senior management
    (B) Customer
    (C) Product manager
    (D) CIO

29. The Project Manager has defined the risks for the project, performed probability and impact analysis and assigned risk owners to the risks. As the project management plan evolves, where will this information end up?

    (A) Risk trigger
    (B) Risk list
    (C) Risk response
    (D) Risk register

30. The Project Manager and team are planning an Internet search engine software project. They are discussing what could go differently than anticipated on the project. They are also trying to identify indicators that could warn them of potential issues. What are these indicators called?

    (A) Triggers
    (B) Risk analysis
    (C) Risks
    (D) Problem solving

31. You are a Project Manager of a home remodeling project. The Budget At Completion (BAC) for this project is $68,000 US. By looking at your schedule, you should be 65% complete, but you are only 50% done. What is your Earned Value?

    (A) $30,800 US
    (B) $44,200 US
    (C) $34,000 US
    (D) $22,000 US

32. Leads and lags can cause delays and acceleration in a schedule. This can be helpful when the goals of the schedule change. Which of the following is the best example of a Lag?

    (A) The earliest a new Ethernet switch can be ordered from the manufacturer
    (B) The latest a telephone system can be ordered from the manufacturer without delaying the project
    (C) The need for concrete to cure an additional day because of the weather before painting the parking lines.
    (D) The critical path

33. The Project Manager is involved in decomposition of the scope of the project. Which of the following will they create as a result of this?

    (A) Risk Breakdown Structure
    (B) Resource breakdown structure
    (C) Work breakdown structure
    (D) Bill of materials

34. Which of the following is created as a result of initiating a road expansion project?

    (A) A signed contract
    (B) Assignment of the Project Manager
    (C) Corrective Action
    (D) Work Results

35. Ranking risks is performed in which of the following?

    (A) Perform Qualitative Risk Analysis
    (B) Expected monetary value (EMV)
    (C) Workarounds
    (D) Risk Triggers

36. The Project Manager is adding people to her staff for the satellite television project. She is presently discussing salary, working hours, location, and benefits. What is the key tool she is utilizing?

    (A) Organizational chart
    (B) Negotiations
    (C) Project team directory
    (D) Staffing Management Plan

37. The company has been plagued by disorganized projects that are not in alignment with business goals, and not focused on interactivity between the projects where applicable. They want to have a better focus on grouping related projects together by business unit and product lines to help maximize efficiency and profitability. Which of the following best describes what they are trying to accomplish?

    (A) Management by Objectives
    (B) Portfolio Management
    (C) Project Management
    (D) Operations Management

38. The Internet marketing project is evaluating the size of their market, time limitations for product life cycle, revenue potential, and number of people available for the project. These are examples of what?

    (A) Assumptions
    (B) Constraints
    (C) Economic consumption
    (D) Strategic planning

39. The project is going through Quality Control. What will the Project Manager use to compare what was created to what was planned?

    (A) Checklists
    (B) Inspection
    (C) Acceptance decisions
    (D) Rework

40. All the following are needed for creating the Scope Management Plan except...

    (A) Project Charter
    (B) Project Management Plan
    (C) Project Scope Statement
    (D) Work Breakdown Structure

41. A Project Manager has completed the Collect Requirements process. The customer has shortened the schedule by six weeks and decided that the Work Breakdown Structure (WBS) be modified. The Project Manager informs the customer that, by modifying the WBS, the project could be subjected to many problems. Which of the following would not be considered a problem of modifying the WBS?

    (A) Budget is not well defined.
    (B) Project may be subject to unforeseen delays.
    (C) There are constant changes to the project.
    (D) Project justification and objectives are not defined.

42.   A risk register that is part of the Project Management Plan on a project would be viewed as what type of communication?

(A) Formal
(B) Contract
(C) Verbal
(D) Formal Written

43.   Your company is evaluating two projects for consideration. Project A has a 40% probability of a $3,000 US loss and a 60% probability of a $20,000 US gain. Project B has a 30% probability of a $5,000 US loss and a 70% probability of a $15,000 US gain. Which of the projects would you select based on the greatest expected monetary value?

(A) Project A
(B) Project B
(C) Project A and B are of even value
(D) The expected monetary value is not high enough on either to make a selection

44.   The customer has requested a five-week delay on the project while the company has winter holiday. This delay was not planned, but the union forced the issue. The company has limited resources. What is the best way to make up the five-week slip?

(A) Put more resources on the project
(B) Crashing
(C) Fast tracking
(D) Perform integrated change control

45.   A contract is a legal agreement between a buyer and seller. There are five components of a contract. Capacity and Consideration are two of five components. All the following would be needed to have a legal contract except…

(A) Legal Purpose
(B) Negotiation
(C) An Offer
(D) Acceptance

46.   The Crosswind network studio has recently been awarded a large contract to create a new children's television show. This will require the company to move into a new office complete with production facilities 300% larger than what it presently has. The schedule is tight for this new project, and there can be no delay. The new facility is behind schedule with the studio and production facilities on pace to finish four months late. The company is attempting to validate data. If this delay proves imminent, it plans to move in temporarily with a partner of theirs with the infrastructure that will meet its needs until the building is complete. This is an example of what type of risk response?

(A) Mitigate
(B) Transfer
(C) Accept
(D) Avoid

47. Crosswind Custom Homes is building a customer's dream house. However, the electrical contractor is unavailable because they are attending a trade show in Las Vegas. This causes a delay in the completion of the house. This is an example of what?

   (A) Crashing
   (B) External dependencies
   (C) Lag
   (D) Mandatory dependencies

48. A project you have been managing is significantly behind schedule. You have received approval to crash the project by adding three resources. The cost you have negotiated is $80 US per hour per resource. The resources will work on the schedule until it is back on track, then the contract will end. What type of contract is this?

   (A) Cost Plus
   (B) Purchase Order
   (C) Time and Materials
   (D) Fixed Price

49. The team is involved in determining what is needed to have the quality process capture the intended results of the testing of the product. This is known as what?

   (A) Quality Management Planning
   (B) Quality Assurance
   (C) Measuring the output of the project
   (D) Quality Control

50. Your DVD training project is almost complete. You have outsourced the DVD creation to an out-of-state company to complete. As the project closes down, what will be completed last?

   (A) Release of resources
   (B) Closing the Project
   (C) Close Procurements
   (D) Assignment of contracts for the next phase

51. The Project Manager is hosting her first bidder's conference. Which of the following should she be sure to not be involved in at the bidder's conference?

   (A) Assurance that vendors have a clear, common understanding of the procurement
   (B) Opportunity for vendors to inquire about the procurement
   (C) Opportunity for vendors to respond to questions that have been incorporated into the procurement document
   (D) Opportunity for vendors to inquire about the bids of other sellers

52. You are the Project Manager working with the customer on a construction project. You are required to purchase and integrate a wireless communication system throughout the construction. A contract is signed with a vendor and work has begun. Half way through the project, the customer decides to upgrade the equipment. This change will require changes to the signed contract. Who has the authority to change the contract?

    (A) Project Manager
    (B) Sponsor
    (C) Contract Administrator
    (D) Customer

53. The project has had some challenges with personnel contribution on the project. The Project Manager feels the team isn't motivated and constantly has to tell them what to do and make sure that the team stays focused. This is an example of what?

    (A) Theory Y environment
    (B) Bad performance
    (C) Theory Z environment
    (D) Theory X environment

54. You are the chief Project Manager of the PMO with your company. Your job is to analyze projects when they close and validate the effectiveness of the project effort. The project closing could be the result of when a project is complete or by any other means. When would you expect to close a project?

    (A) When a project runs out of money
    (B) All the answers
    (C) When a project completes scope verification
    (D) When a project is cancelled

55. The mortgage company is building an application processing center for its new home equity division. Given that this is its first venture utilizing this new type of business, a number of new processes have been created to ensure compliance with various regulatory issues. Which of the following would help verify that these processes are being accomplished?

    (A) Quality audit
    (B) Control chart
    (C) Process flow
    (D) Checklist

56. The team is in the process of determining what the customer needs for the office update project, focusing on discovering and procuring products based on the customer-defined requirements. What is this called?

    (A) Meeting the customers needs
    (B) Scope verification
    (C) Definition of quality
    (D) Qualitative analysis

57. Task A is worth $500, is 80% complete, and actually cost $500. Task B is worth $450, is 75% complete, and actually cost $402 so far. Task C is worth $600, is 90% complete, and has cost $550 so far. The total budget is $3000. What is the cost performance index for the tasks listed?

   (A) 1.10
   (B) 1.11
   (C) 0.88
   (D) 0.84

58. You are a Project Manager starting negotiations with a vendor. As the vendor is attempting to maximize the value of the contract they are negotiating all the following are negotiation strategies they could use except...

   (A) Force Majeure
   (B) Lying
   (C) Deadline
   (D) Withdrawal

59. You are doing some analysis associated with project selection. There is a lot of debate concerning which projects to select. You have the following to choose from: Project A with an Internal Rate of Return (IRR) of 18.2%, Project B with an Internal Rate of Return (IRR) of 21%, Project C with an Internal Rate of Return (IRR) of 13%, and Project D with an Internal Rate of Return (IRR) of 9%. If you can select only one project, which do you choose?

   (A) Project A
   (B) Project B
   (C) Project C
   (D) Project D

60. John has been assigned to watch for certain events associated with his area of expertise on the project and was told to implement responses from the risk register if any of these events occur. Which of the following roles is John performing on the project?

   (A) Risk Seeker
   (B) Team Lead
   (C) Project Manager
   (D) Risk Owner

61. Which of the following best describes the lowest level of decomposition for the Work Breakdown Structure (WBS)?

   (A) Breaking down work where it's budgeted and scheduled
   (B) Breaking down work where it's completely and clearly defined
   (C) Breaking down work where the bottom levels of the WBS represent work packages
   (D) Breaking down work where it's budgeted, scheduled and completely and clearly defined

62. The contract administrator is involved in determining the state of a contract that is nearing closure. In what process group is the Contract Administrator working?

    (A) Closing
    (B) Planning
    (C) Execution
    (D) Monitoring and Controlling

63. Crosswind Custom Homes is building a customer's dream house. However, rain has delayed the finish by two weeks. The Project Manager is evaluating options to make up the lost time. After discussing the various options with Senior Management, the Project Manager has decided to fast track the project. By doing so, the Project Manager could be adding what to the project?

    (A) Scope change
    (B) Risk
    (C) Time change
    (D) Responsibility

64. Calculate the variance for the following: Pessimistic=50, Optimistic=10, Realistic=24.

    (A) 55.55
    (B) 26
    (C) Not enough information
    (D) 44.44

65. A movie theatre construction project is going relatively well, but the people doing work on the project are complaining about reporting to two different people, each with conflicting agendas. This is an example of what type of project environment?

    (A) Functional
    (B) Matrix
    (C) Tight Matrix
    (D) Projectized

66. The advertising agency has been awarded a $54M US, 8-year contract to manage the advertising campaigns of a fast food chicken restaurant. The company realizes that this work is going to require a specific skill set for 40 people. Their current workforce only has seven people with this skill set. This skill set is somewhat rare and specialized in the area they are located. They have chosen to buy a company much smaller than they are, but this company's core focus is this type of skill set. The company employs 50 people with this skill set. This is an example of what type of risk response strategy?

    (A) Mitigate
    (B) Accept
    (C) Exploit
    (D) Share

67. The Project Management team has just completed the process of creating risk categories for the risks on the road construction project and is displaying the risks in a graphical format to help team members have a better understanding of what could happen on the project. They have identified among other things regulatory, supplies, labor, external and internal areas where they could have issues. What have they created?

    (A) Risk Management Plan
    (B) Risk Breakdown Structure
    (C) Risk Register
    (D) Prioritized list of quantified risks

68. In the communication model, who is responsible if the message is delivered in a confusing and misinterpreted way?

    (A) Receiver
    (B) Both the sender and receiver
    (C) Project Manager
    (D) Sender

69. What is the most accurate benefit below for using a work authorization system?

    (A) To show who is responsible for what work
    (B) To show what work is to be done in the project
    (C) To serve as a time-tracking system
    (D) To help ensure that work is done in the appropriate sequence

70. The project planning is progressing on budget. The Project Manager and the team meet regularly and are ready to begin updating the project planning documents with a major scope change. What input into the planning process will help the team the most?

    (A) WBS
    (B) Project Management Plan
    (C) Risk list
    (D) Network diagram

71. The Project Manager is creating an estimate for raised flooring in a data center. The project has six different bids from six vendors. Two of the bids are $4.00/sq. ft higher than the Project Manager would like to pay. Two of the other bids are $0.25 higher, but fall within the project's cost range of plus or minus 10%. Which of the following types of estimates is the Project Manager using?

    (A) Gut Feel
    (B) Bottom up
    (C) Parametric
    (D) Analogous

72. You are in the process of defining the quality standards for the clothing catalog project. You have defined the variables to measure regarding the catalog and determined what attributes are required to achieve the impact your marketing plan has defined. Which of the following is not an attribute?

    (A) Depth
    (B) Inches
    (C) Kilometers
    (D) Pounds

73. The team is involved in planning risk management. They are trying to establish an overall project risk ranking for the project. This will allow them to evaluate the project compared to others in the portfolio they are managing. What process did they just complete?

    (A) Perform Qualitative Risk Analysis
    (B) Identify Risks
    (C) Monitor and Control Risks
    (D) Risk Mitigation

74. The airline reservation project has been relatively stable. The Cost Performance Index is presently 0.91 and the schedule performance index is 0.87. Risk could have been managed better from the start of this project. 60% through the execution of the project management plan, the Project Manager assigned a person to do nothing but monitor for risks and work with the people who will implement the risk response plans. What are these people called?

    (A) Sponsor
    (B) Risk-Averse
    (C) Project Manager
    (D) Risk Owners

75. Calculate expected monetary value of the following: 0.4 probability of $5000 US, 0.3 probability of $3800 US, 0.2 probability of -$2700 US, 0.1 probability of $3000 US.

    (A) $3,800 US
    (B) $5,000 US
    (C) $2900 US
    (D) -$2,700 US

76. Calculate the PERT estimate for the following: Pessimistic=50, Optimistic=10, Realistic=24.

    (A) Not enough information
    (B) 26
    (C) 15
    (D) 16.67

77. What organization could audit projects in an organization to help ensure the health of the project and offer suggestions for improvement if needed?

    (A) Projectized Organization
    (B) Balanced Matrix Organization
    (C) Tight Matrixed Organization
    (D) Project Management Office

78. Task A is worth $500, is 80% complete, and actually cost $500. Task B is worth $450, is 75% complete, and actually cost $402 so far. Task C is worth $600, is 90% complete, and has cost $550 so far. The total budget is $3000. What is the Variance at Completion for the tasks listed?

    (A) -$409.09
    (B) $3000
    (C) $409.09
    (D) $1957.09

79. Crosswind Custom Development is building a customer's network infrastructure. However, a shipping delay will cause the equipment to arrive three weeks late. The Project Manager evaluates the schedule and determines that by crashing the project, it could be placed back on schedule by compressing the deployment of the equipment. After discussing this with senior management, the Project Manager has decided to crash the project. By doing so, the Project Manager is adding what to the project?

    (A) Responsibility
    (B) Time change
    (C) Scope Change
    (D) Cost change

80. You are a Project Manager trying to estimate the duration of a project. You would like to use an Activity on Arrow diagram as your Network diagram. You decide to use an estimating method with three activities: Optimistic, Pessimistic, and Most Holistic. What estimating method would you use?

    (A) PERT
    (B) CPM
    (C) GERT
    (D) None of the above

81. The project team has just started planning as a result of the charter being signed. The charter provides all the following except...

    (A) Defines the Scope Statement
    (B) Outlines the Project Manager's authority
    (C) Contains or makes reference to the product description
    (D) Gives the project existence

82. Which of the following would a team create as a result of using a Change Control System?

    (A) Change requests
    (B) Approved changes
    (C) Impact analysis
    (D) Signoff

83. The project team is planning an upgrade to a client's movie production studio. During planning, the team members discover that the lab where the editing processes are to reside will not have sufficient space, forcing the client to lease another building. This building will also be shared with another department. What type of Cost would this be?

    (A) Direct
    (B) Indirect
    (C) Variable
    (D) Indirect Fixed

84. The project is going well until a Stakeholder requests a significant change based on a modification in the Stakeholder's business process. After meeting with the team to determine impact it appears that the change will likely double the length of the project because of the complexity associated with the change. The change request and its impact analysis are going before the Change Control Board (CCB) for review and potential approval. What is the purpose of the Change Control Board (CCB)?

    (A) To work with the Change Control Manager for analyzing changes
    (B) To analyze changes that are requested for the project
    (C) To eliminate as many changes as possible on the project
    (D) To control change by approval of needed changes and rejection of unneeded changes to the project

85. To develop a CDMA base station for your company, a project requires some new test equipment and a new D++ complier. The finance department explains that this is a capital purchase to be depreciated using the sum of the years digits. This is an example of what?

    (A) Standard Depreciation
    (B) Accelerated Depreciation
    (C) Fixed Direct Cost
    (D) Straight-line Depreciation

86. Which of the following would a Project Manager use to track cost related activities on a project?

    (A) Cost management plan
    (B) Work Breakdown Structure
    (C) Control Costs
    (D) Budget management plan

87. The project planning for the trade show is progressing on schedule. The Project Manager and the team are meeting to begin cost estimating. The Sponsor has said that estimates must be very accurate. Which of the following estimating techniques will provide the most accuracy?

(A) Bottom up estimating
(B) Cost estimating
(C) Parametric estimating
(D) Analogous estimating

88. The advertising agency has been awarded a $20M US contract to provide consulting and support services to a restaurant chain in creating an advertising campaign. If things go well, they will get the next phase of the project that will include world wide advertising. The advertising agency is relatively small, and this contract is bigger than anything they have been awarded to date. To ensure that they can effectively complete the contract, and not jeopardize their other work they have chosen to partner with another company to do the work. This is an example of what type of risk response strategy?

(A) Mitigate
(B) Accept
(C) Exploit
(D) Share

89. The Project Manager is reviewing testing output data from the NUBUS system. Generally, the data looks good other than one issue. He observes seven consecutive data points on one side of the mean in three areas on the control chart. What is this called?

(A) Acceptable measurements
(B) Too loose of specification limits
(C) A violation of the Seven Run Rule
(D) Lucky seven gets eleven

90. A marketing campaign is being built to support a new product at a utility company. The company doesn't have data on what volume to expect from the marketing campaign and the associated advertising. This data is important because it will help drive the number of employees needed department so customers' needs can be met. The Project Manager remembers that a similar project was by a company his company acquired. He begins to review data from this project. This is a best example of what?

(A) Historical Information
(B) Lessons Learned
(C) Constraints
(D) Assumptions

91. The client has requested a four-week delay on the project while the company remodels its training facilities. This delay wasn't planned, but the facilities were going to be shut down by the safety board for various violations. The company is limited with its resource options and will have to make up the work quickly. This delay will be best shown in what?

    (A) Responsibility Assignment Matrix (RAM)
    (B) Network diagram
    (C) Budget
    (D) Work Breakdown Structure (WBS)

92. The software development company has recently been awarded a large contract to create a new animation software program. This will require the company to move into a new office complete with production facilities twice their current size. The schedule is tight for this new project. The new facility is behind schedule with the cubicles and network wiring on pace to finish three weeks late. If this can't be done on time and will slip three weeks, the company has decided there is nothing it can do, and it will simply deal with the consequences. This is an example of what type of risk response?

    (A) Accept
    (B) Avoid
    (C) Mitigate
    (D) Transfer

93. A Project Manager was assigned to manage a project to develop pink widgets for the Project Manager's company. The project will cost the company $510,000 over the next 12 months. It is projected that the widgets will earn the company $37,500 per month. How much time will it take to recover the cost for this project?

    (A) 18 months
    (B) Not enough information
    (C) 10 months
    (D) 14 months

94. The development team is building a new video creation product. This is a new product type at their company, and the market for the product is volatile and changing every three months. According to the product manager a key to success will be the ability to evolve the planning as more information about the market is discovered, but there could be fluctuation in the direction of the development. Which type of scheduling approach best fits this need?

    (A) Crashing
    (B) Rolling wave planning
    (C) Precedence diagramming
    (D) Fast Tracking

95. The team implemented a risk response plan when a vendor was unable to fulfill a contract commitment for a training class. The response was to choose another vendor. However, in this type of training, it's hard to find a good company, and the one selected doesn't have a much better reputation. The new company is somewhat better at meeting the terms of the contract, but still has some issues from time to time, which is no surprise. What best describes these issues?

    (A) Secondary risk
    (B) Workaround
    (C) Residual risk
    (D) Risk response plan

96. The Project Management Team is working in the executing and monitoring/controlling phases of the project. There are four sponsors and 34 Stakeholders on the project. Which of the following is the most likely to focus on communication at this point in the project to ensure the project achieves the quality standards established in planning?

    (A) During planning revisions
    (B) In negotiating the Project Manager assignment
    (C) When the Change Control Board (CCB) meets
    (D) At key interface points where the various work packages come together

97. In performing management of the project, the Project Manager spends a large percentage of her time communicating. Which of the following is the best advantage of doing this on the project?

    (A) A Theory Y management style
    (B) An accurate communication management plan
    (C) A detailed project file
    (D) A greater emphasis on successful integration of the various pieces of the project

98. Which of the following would a Project Manager use to evaluate a hurricane that hit the data center on a project? The Project Manager would use which of the following to compensate for the loss from the hurricane?

    (A) Risk management
    (B) Schedule Reserves
    (C) Management Reserves
    (D) Contingency Reserves

99. The construction project is almost finished. The team is involved in many different activities to close the project. The team members are in the process of creating project archives. All the following are examples of project archives except...

    (A) Contracts
    (B) Financial records
    (C) Negotiations parameters
    (D) Internal project documentation

100. A Project Manager has decided to outsource the installation of an electrical security system in their business offices. The buyer has given specific details to the vendor on the schedule and cost of each site. This will also be a fixed price contract. What type of Scope of work is being provided to the sellers?

    (A) Time and Material
    (B) Functionality
    (C) Design
    (D) Scope Statement

101. A Project Manager has completed the Define Scope process. The customer and Sponsor have shortened the schedule by eight weeks and decided that the work breakdown structure will be cut in half. What would be the best action the Project Manager should take?

    (A) Call a meeting and notify the team of the change in schedule
    (B) Discuss with the customer and Sponsor the ramifications of having the WBS not reflect the true work of the project.
    (C) Begin execution of the project
    (D) Provide the customer and Sponsor an updated schedule and budget

102. A contract administrator would use all the following as contracts except...

    (A) Purchase Order
    (B) Agreement
    (C) Proposal
    (D) Memorandum of Understanding

103. Calculate the standard deviation for the following: Pessimistic=50, Optimistic=10, Realistic=24.

    (A) 26
    (B) Not enough information
    (C) 5.67
    (D) 6.667

104. You are a Project Manager trying to decide what quality approach to implement at your company. You have decided that it is in the best interest of the company to do testing while in the developing phase to get immediate feedback. You also decide to include statistical analysis for evaluating the output data. This philosophy is known as...

    (A) Quality Assurance
    (B) Quality Management Plan
    (C) Total Quality Management
    (D) ISO 9000 Quality System

105. A project will be using a vendor to install computer network wiring in a three story shopping center. The buyer is asking vendors to describe how they will do this work and how much it will cost. What type of document will be used to solicit this information?

    (A) Request for Information (RFI)
    (B) Request for Proposal (RFP)
    (C) Invitation for Bid (IFB)
    (D) Request for Quote (RFQ)

106. The Project Management Team is creating the Quality Management Plan. The Sponsor has told them to focus on not having to redo things, and to try to do things on the project that will help the project get done efficiently and increate profits from the product of the project. What best describes what the Sponsor is asking for?

    (A) TQM
    (B) Kaizen
    (C) Zero defects
    (D) Fitness for Use

107. Which of the following would a contract administrator use if they are using a unilateral contract?

    (A) Time and Material
    (B) Cost Plus
    (C) Statement of Work
    (D) Purchase Order

108. Which of the following can the new Project Manager use to see what the reporting relationships are on her new data cleansing project?

    (A) Resource histogram
    (B) Staffing Management Plan
    (C) Organizational Breakdown Structure (OBS)
    (D) Responsibility Assignment Matrix

109. Which of the roles would control resources in a balanced matrix environment?

    (A) Sponsor
    (B) Project management
    (C) Functional management
    (D) Senior management

110. A Project Manager is assigned to a project that is in the design phase of creating a BBX transceiver. The Project Manager is in the process of reviewing work completed to gain Formal Acceptance. This is known as what?

    (A) Verify Scope
    (B) Control Scope
    (C) Quality Assurance
    (D) Quality Control

111. The shirt printing company has added a new line for its silk screening business. It involves new technology to build printed images on the shirts quickly and cheaper. The company anticipates that this new technology will allow it to make a more efficient yield from the printing process. The company is also increasing the amount of insurance it has on its main facility because there has been flooding in the area in recent years from excessive rain. Adding this insurance is an example of what?

(A) ISO 9000
(B) Conformance to quality
(C) Business risk
(D) Insurable risk

112. Task A is worth $500, is 80% complete, and actually cost $500. Task B is worth $450, is 75% complete, and actually cost $402 so far. Task C is worth $600, is 90% complete, and has cost $550 so far. The total budget is $3000. What is the schedule variance for the tasks listed?

(A) $0.84
(B) $174.5
(C) -$272.50
(D) $272.5

113. The Project Manager is creating an estimate for building a company workout facility. It is something that is new to the Project Manager and he wants to make sure all the work of the project is covered. He decides to create a Bottom-Up estimate. All the following are advantages of this type of estimate except...

(A) It provides team buy in when they help create it.
(B) It provides supporting detail of the estimate.
(C) It has a greater degree of accuracy because of the detail at which it was created.
(D) It takes a great amount of time to create.

114. In reviewing the benefits and challenges of a Projectized, Matrix and Functional Organization, which of the following is considered an advantage of a Functional Organization?

(A) Optimization for a single focus on the project
(B) Business unit competency
(C) Having a place to go when the project starts
(D) Having to obtain approval from project management

115. The Project Manager has scheduled weekly status meetings with the team and three customer contacts. The meetings have been disorganized with people addressing their own needs and taking longer than needed on unplanned items with no discipline. Which of the following would improve the meetings?

(A) Create and publish an agenda
(B) Create and publish an agenda, and establish the leader of the meeting
(C) Send the team to communication training
(D) Determine who is in charge of the meeting

116. Which of the following is not a regulation?

    (A) The documented way to dispose of old paint
    (B) The zoning for an industrial area
    (C) The average number of losing lottery tickets in a week
    (D) The building code for a city

117. Which of the following does the Project Manager need to create a variance report?

    (A) Baseline measurements
    (B) Status reports
    (C) Change request
    (D) Project archives

118. You are the Project Manager on an oil pipeline project. Due to the rough terrain, the scope of the project had to be modified to compensate for the required drilling and excavating changes. You need to verify that these changes have been put in place. What would best help you determine this?

    (A) Project Scope Statement updates
    (B) Scope Changes
    (C) Scope Management Plan
    (D) Control Scope System

119. You are the Project Manager for a consumer research database project. You have just finished putting together all the various plans into an integrated complete document that the team will use to guide them in creating the project work. What step have you just completed?

    (A) Project Management Plan execution
    (B) Developing the Project Management Plan
    (C) Charter signoff
    (D) Develop Schedule

120. The Project Manager is performing risk management on a project. She is reviewing risk triggers in the Risk Register. All the following are accurate about risk triggers except...

    (A) A trigger comes before a risk.
    (B) A trigger does not mean a risk will occur.
    (C) A trigger is an indicator that a risk event will occur.
    (D) A trigger is an indicator that a risk event could occur.

121. You are the Project Manager of an engineering project for a cellular base station with a one-year schedule as defined by the project management plan. You need a spectrum analyzer. During the procurement process, you have decided to rent this equipment. The rental cost is $506 per month. What type of cost is this?

    (A) Direct
    (B) Indirect
    (C) Variable
    (D) Fixed

122. In evaluating slack on a project which of the following formulas can a Project Manager use to calculate it?

    (A) Late Finish-Early Finish (LF-EF)
    (B) Late Finish- Early Start (LF-ES)
    (C) Late Finish- Late Start (LF-LS)
    (D) Early Finish- Late Start (EF-LS)

123. A project will be using a vendor to purchase broadcast cameras and computers for a call center for a television channel run by a foreign government. The government has requested a proposal from prospective sellers of the equipment. What type of document is being provided to the sellers?

    (A) Invitation for Bid (IFB)
    (B) Request for Quote (RFQ)
    (C) Request for Information (RFI)
    (D) Request for Proposal (RFP)

124. You are doing risk management on a project, discussing with the sponsor the probabilities of finishing the project on schedule. What must the sum of all probabilities equal?

    (A) 99.9997%
    (B) 100%
    (C) 99.73%
    (D) 68.26%

125. The electronics project is going through planning to create a less costly version of an existing product. In evaluating the Triple Constraint, which of the following is the highest priority?

    (A) Scope
    (B) Time
    (C) Cost
    (D) They are all equal unless otherwise stated in the charter.

126. The marketing project is on schedule and under budget. The customer is pleased, but would like to add a few features. As a result, a new team is brought in to help the existing team implement this additional work. Before the team arrives, Senior Management would like to see where the project stands. Which of the following do you show them?

    (A) Gantt chart
    (B) Network diagram
    (C) Work Breakdown Structure
    (D) Milestone chart

127. Task A is worth $500, is 80% complete, and actually cost $500. Task B is worth $450, is 75% complete, and actually cost $402 so far. Task C is worth $600, is 90% complete, and has cost $550 so far. The total budget is $3000. What is the total Earned Value for the tasks listed?

    (A) $1452
    (B) $1277.5
    (C) $1550
    (D) $3000

128. The Sponsor is reviewing two different projects for approval. It has determined that the company has enough resources to do only one project. Project A is worth $800,000 US and Project B is worth $1,650,000. What is the Opportunity Cost of selecting Project B?

    (A) $1,650,000 US
    (B) $800,000 US
    (C) $850,000 US
    (D) Not enough information

129. You are the Project Manager on the development of a RAID 4 computer storage network. The customer has been very concerned about the correctness and acceptance of the work results as they have had corrupt data in the past and the goal is to have this serve as a backup system. You are not sure what the customer is saying about the "correctness and acceptance" so you review your *PMBOK®* Guide. What areas below will likely be involved in attaining what the government is concerned about?

    (A) Control Scope and Verify Scope
    (B) Administrative Closure and Quality Assurance
    (C) Plan Quality and Quality Control
    (D) Verify Scope and Quality Control

130. In evaluating a make or buy analysis of services needed all the following are reasons for outsourcing work except...

    (A) Your company doesn't possess the skills needed for the work.
    (B) Labor rates in the foreign countries are comparable to your company's labor rate.
    (C) Your company isn't concerned about protecting the information associated with the work.
    (D) Your company doesn't have excess capacity for the work.

131. Task A is worth $500, is 80% complete, and actually cost $500. Task B is worth $450, is 75% complete, and actually cost $402 so far. Task C is worth $600, is 90% complete, and has cost $550 so far. The total budget is $3000. What is the cost variance for the tasks listed?

    (A) -$174.50
    (B) $174.50
    (C) $0.84
    (D) $272.5

132. A Project Manager is beginning the solicitation process to find companies that can potentially provide the needed services. The buyer wants to consider only sellers of the services that have done projects of greater than $20M US and have employees with a high level security clearance. What screening mechanism is this?

    (A) Advertising
    (B) Bidders Conference
    (C) Weighting System
    (D) Qualified Seller List

133. The Project Manager is in the process of closing the project and plans a meeting with the team to document and discuss how the project went. This activity is known as what?

    (A) Lessons Learned
    (B) Project reports
    (C) Report Performance
    (D) Project archives

134. The Sponsor on the airport runway project has just told the Project Manager, about a change he wants. He says that the change will cost 20% less and should not cause any problems to the existing environment. Which of the following should concern the Project Manager the most?

    (A) Schedule impact
    (B) Scope impact
    (C) Scope and Schedule impact
    (D) Quality impact

135. A Project Manager is in the process of using a rolling wave planning approach and documenting the project work. With help for the product description, the Project Manager has defined the Scope Statement for the project. What process is the Project Manager performing?

    (A) Collect Requirements
    (B) Define Scope
    (C) Verify Scope
    (D) Control Scope

136. Home Creation store is starting to use Just in Time inventory because its inventory costs are greater than the industry average. The company feels this policy will help minimize inventory costs and be more efficient. What is the amount of inventory needed for this type of process?

    (A) Warehouse capacity
    (B) 25%
    (C) Zero
    (D) Minimal

137. The project team is working together on the airport runway addition project. The Project Manager has delivered a report that describes how much work should have been accomplished, how much work is actually accomplished, and the actual cost to complete the work. The Project Manager plans to use this report to show the state of the schedule and budget. What type of report is this?

    (A) Status report
    (B) Progress report
    (C) Variance report
    (D) Earned Value report

138. You are in the initial phase of a project and are doing an estimate for a project that requires a MRI lab for a hospital to be built. What is the estimate range you would use for this project?

    (A) -10% to +25%
    (B) -25% to +75%
    (C) -5% to +10%
    (D) -25% to +85%

139. The project team has begun development on a project in a new market for their company. Because the market is so unstable, the product they are creating doesn't necessarily have all the details defined before planning begins. The team has to plan as much as possible and begin the work. As they learn more about the work, they will adapt their planning. Which of the following best describes the approach?

    (A) Progressive elaboration
    (B) Extreme programming
    (C) Total Quality Management
    (D) Project management

140. The quality improvement project is doing procurement audits. It is identifying successes and failures of the procurement process. This identification is important for Formal Acceptance and Closure. What process is the project in?

    (A) Closing
    (B) Quality Assurance
    (C) Close Procurements
    (D) Close Project or Phase

141. The Crosswind broadcasting has recently been awarded a large contract to create a new children's television show. This will require the company to move into a new office complete with production facilities 300% larger than what it presently has. The schedule is tight for this new project, and there can be no delay. The new facility is behind schedule with the sets and production facilities on pace to finish two months late. The company is trying to use an incentive fee to motivate the provider of these services to complete the work as quickly as possible even if it results in a smaller delay. This is an example of what type of risk response?

    (A) Accept
    (B) Mitigate
    (C) Transfer
    (D) Avoid

142. You are the Project Manager for a national satellite rollout project. You are required to purchase and integrate reporting software for all the retail stores. As the Project Manager, you want one price from the vendors for the purchase and implementation of this product. What type of document should be used?

    (A) Request for Quote
    (B) Request for Information
    (C) Request for Proposal
    (D) Invitation for Bid

143. You are testing what the team has created on the project. You are trying to determine if a project is producing a low quality or low-grade product. Which statement best describes the differences?

    (A) Low quality may not be a problem, but low grade is always a problem.
    (B) Products can have low quality but high grade.
    (C) Products can have high quality but low grade.
    (D) Low quality is always a problem, but low grade may not.

144. The project management plan contains all the following except…

    (A) The change control system
    (B) Staffing management plan
    (C) The schedule
    (D) Corrective action

145. The Project Manager is creating an estimate for an electrical sub-system that is being built. The customer is now creating his budget for the next two calendar years and needs this estimate as soon as possible. A Senior Project Manager has managed many projects that included building sub-systems and is considered an expert. You solicit his help on the estimate. Which of the following types of estimates is the Project Manager using?

    (A) Parametric
    (B) Analogous
    (C) Delphi Technique
    (D) Bottom up

146. The project has five people on it. Four more are added. What is the total number of communication channels added to the project?

    (A) 36 Channels
    (B) 6 Channels
    (C) 15 channels
    (D) 26 Channels

147. The Project Manager and team have completed the project Scope within budget, but behind schedule, and have just received signoff from the customer. What is this activity called?

    (A) Formal Acceptance
    (B) Verify Scope
    (C) Project archives
    (D) Contract closeout

148. The company is in the testing phase of its software project, tracking defects that come in from premium customers who are testing the beta version of the project work. Given the nature of a new project, a variety of defects is being discovered over time. Which of the following will the team use to evaluate this data graphically?

    (A) Pareto chart
    (B) Flowchart
    (C) Run Chart
    (D) Fishbone diagram

149. According to the *PMBOK® Guide - Fourth Edition*, where does Estimate Activity Resources occur?

    (A) Scope
    (B) Human Resources
    (C) Time
    (D) Procurement

150. The team is involved in creating the Project Management Plan. They are in the process of evaluating risks that could occur on the project. Which of the following best describes project risk?

    (A) It can be either a negative or positive event.
    (B) It can be something that has already happened.
    (C) It can be a negative event only.
    (D) It can be a positive event only.

Full CAPM® Exam Simulation Answer Key

1. Project planning is ongoing as the team analyzes how long it will take to process a new order and a change order through the new call center. This analysis will help them determine how many employees to have in the call center based on their demand as anticipated by customer volume. This is an example of what?

    Correct Answer: (A) Assumptions
    Explanation: Assumptions are educated guesses made on the project about items that are not known. Constraints are variables that can limit the options available for the project and typically deal with resources, time, or money. The other two answers are noise.

2. The Project Manager and her team are involved in establishing the costs of the project and applying it to the schedule to determine when these costs will happen on the project. Which of the following are they doing?

    Correct Answer: (A) Determine Budget
    Explanation: Determine Budget involves applying costs to the individual work packages or tasks along with the schedule to establish a cost baseline for measuring project performance. The Estimate Costs process involves getting a high level cost estimate for the overall project. Control Costs involves managing the costs of the project. Cost Baseline is the output of Determine Budget.

3. In performing a project, the team will focus on the project life cycle and the project management life cycle. What are the five phases of a Project Management Life Cycle (PMLC)?

    Correct Answer: (D) Initiating, Planning, Executing, Monitoring and Controlling, Closing
    Explanation: Per the *PMBOK® Guide - Fourth Edition*, the process groups that make up the PMI methodology or "Project Management Life Cycle" are Initiating, Planning, Executing, Monitoring and Controlling, Closing. It is not uncommon for these process groups to be considered phases of a project.

4. The Project Manager is considering quitting his job to develop a book, and supporting products for the PMP® Exam, an idea he created outside his job. If it sells well, he plans to start his own company and sell them full time. What characteristic is he showing toward risk?

    Correct Answer: (A) Risk Seeker
    Explanation: A Risk Seeker mentality is that of looking for the big reward and being prepared to pay significantly if it's missed. The Risk-Averse mentality is a very conservative approach to risk. A Risk Neutral mentality is somewhere between that of a Risk Seeker and Risk-Averse mentality. The other answer is noise.

5. All the following could be considered functions of the GERT diagramming method except...

    Correct Answer: (B) Some activities may be fast tracked.
    Explanation: Fast tracking is a tool of the Develop Schedule process and is used in duration compression. Fast tracking is not a function of GERT.

6. The planning is progressing on schedule for the hotel renovation project. The Project Manager and the team are ready to begin estimating costs. The customer needs an estimate as soon as possible. What estimating method should the team use?

Correct Answer: (B) Analogous estimating
Explanation: Analogous estimating creates a high estimate with no significant detail. The main advantage of this estimate is that you can create it quickly. In bottom up estimating, the Project Manager and the project team work together to create a complete estimate from the bottom up. Estimate Costs is the process the Project Manager and team are executing.

7. You are a Project Manager assigned to a project that has spent $4,000,000 US. The original budget was $1,500,000. Senior management is considering stopping this project. What term describes the $1,500,000 that has been spent so far?

Correct Answer: (C) Sunk cost
Explanation: Sunk costs are those that have already been spent on the project. They should not be taken into consideration when determining whether to continue the project. Expected Monetary Value (EMV) is the product of probability and impact in Risk Management. The Budgeted Cost of Work Performed (BCWP) is the Earned Value (EV). Opportunity cost does not apply here.

8. The Project Manager is having a team meeting and explaining to the team the upcoming milestones that are due. What are the characteristics of a milestone?

(A) A duration of zero (0)
(B) The completion of a major event in the project
(C) The completion of major deliverables
(D) All the above

Correct Answer: (B) All the above
Explanation: A milestone is a completion of major deliverables, a completion of a major event, and has duration of zero (0). These are all characteristics of a milestone.

9. A new tape backup server has just been purchased for backing up the company's development and release software. The tape backup server costs $50,000 US, and it was necessary to upgrade the local area network with an Ethernet switch at a cost of $10,000. The Project Manager is told that she needs to set up a depreciation schedule for the tape backup server over a five-year period with a value of $0 at the end of this period. She will use standard depreciation in the calculation. What is the amount per year the server will depreciate?

Correct Answer: (B) $10,000 US
Explanation: To calculate depreciation, you must determine a few facts. What is the value of the asset at the end of the schedule? What is the amount of the asset to begin with? What is the number of years of the depreciation schedule? First, subtract the ending value of the asset from the beginning value of the asset ($50K-$0=$50K). Then divide the $50K by the years (5) of the depreciation schedule. This results in $10K per year of depreciation. The question asked for only the depreciation of the tape backup server and not the Ethernet switch.

10. You are doing quality planning on a project. The Sponsor puts into the charter that the quality standard wanted on the project is +/- 2 sigma. This translates to what percentage?

Correct Answer: (A) 95.46%
Explanation: 2 sigma is 95.46%. The percentage for 1 sigma is 68.26%, 3 sigma is 99.73% and 50% is noise.

11. The team has just completed the process of evaluating the success of the data cleansing project. The team members analyzed how the approach to running the project worked. They evaluated the planning and executing. They documented how the Sponsor and Senior Management supported the project as well as the conflicts that were generated by three Functional Managers. What have they just completed?

Correct Answer: (A) Lessons Learned
Explanation: The Lessons Learned is an analysis of how the project went. It includes initiating to closing activities. It documents what worked on the project and what didn't so that the lessons can be learned and the good methods repeated and the bad eliminated. Administrative closure is the process in which Lessons Learned occur. Procurement Audit and Project Closure are noise.

12. Flexibility with an activity on a Network diagram is also known as what?

Correct Answer: (D) Slack
Explanation: Slack and Float are interchangeable terminology. They represent flexibility with an activity before it impact the following activities or finish dates of the project. Lag is a delay between tasks on a Network diagram. GERT and PERT are noise.

13. The Project Manager is working with the customer to gain formal acceptance on the documentation deliverables for a software project. The customer is saying that the deliverables are unusable in their present form as they don't align with the project requirements. Upon reviewing documentation, the customer tells the Project Manager that the requirements are not accurate to meet the needs for which the project was undertaken. Which of the following will help fix this problem?

Correct Answer: (B) Control Scope
Explanation: Control Scope is used to review and approve or reject scope change requests to the project. That would fix the problem in this case. Scope analysis is noise. Team-building would be used to help the group of people on the project become more productive that is not applicable in this situation. Verify Scope helps validate that the project created what it was to create. That is the process that discovered the problem of the difference in scope planned and created.

14. A Project Manager studying different motivation theories is impressed with one theory which states that people are not motivated by money but by self actualization. To what theory is the Project Manager referring?

Correct Answer: (B) Maslow's hierarchy
Explanation: Maslow's hierarchy states that people do not work for money but towards Self-Actualization. McGregor's Theory of X and Y classifies workers into one of two groups. Theory X states that management is in charge and that labor does not want to work. Theory Y states that labor wants to work and requires little supervision. Herzberg's Theory deals with hygiene factors and motivating elements.

15. The team has had five meetings to decompose the work of the aircraft carrier project. They are making progress and in a few more meetings should have all the decomposition complete for the multi year project. All the following are benefits of using a WBS except...

Correct Answer: (D) Identifies special work packages that can be created outside the WBS, but within the project
Explanation: If the work is not in the WBS, it is not part of the project. All other answers represent benefits of using a WBS.

16. A project will be using a company to provide technicians for a distribution center project. Presently, the Project Manager is in contract negotiation with a vendor and the negotiations are going too smooth. In what process is the Project Manager involved?

Correct Answer: (C) Conduct Procurements
Explanation: Conduct Procurements involves receiving and reviewing proposals from companies being considered for the work. Plan Procurements analyzes procurement or outsourcing needs.
Close Procurements validates that the contract terms and conditions have been met.
Administer Procurements involves management of the contract itself.

17. As the buyer is involved in creating Request For Proposals (RFP) for an infrastructure project, they will provide these to sellers of services. All the following are names used for a seller except…

Correct Answer: (B) Acquiring organization
Explanation: The acquiring organization is a name also for the buyer of services. The other names are all names for sellers of services.

18. Crosswind Custom Homes is building a customer's dream house. However, rain has delayed the finish by three weeks. The schedule shows that the next task is to install the windows followed by the outside siding. This is an example of what?

Correct Answer: (A) Mandatory dependencies
Explanation: A mandatory dependency is required, and internal to the organization. An external dependency is a dependency that is out of control of the organization. Crashing and Lag are noise.

19. The Project Manager and Functional Manager are having a disagreement on resource allocation for a new broadband project. The Functional Manager wants the resource for an operational issue that needs attention, and the Project Manager wants the resource to work on the project so it stays on schedule as planned. Which of the following roles can help resolve this problem?

Correct Answer: (D) Senior management
Explanation: Senior management is responsible for a number of areas on a project. The main responsibility is to help support the project and resolve resource conflicts as they occur. For situational questions, assume that you are in a Balanced Matrix environment, unless otherwise stated. This will include Functional Managers controlling resources. The Project Manager's responsibility is to drive the completion of project work. Typically, the Sponsor's responsibility is to pay for the project and own it when it is complete

20. The Project Manager is creating a network diagram to show the sequencing on the project. He is using a method which includes dummies. All the following Network diagram techniques display this dependency except...

Correct Answer: (D) Activity on Node (AON)
Explanation: Activity on Node (AON) doesn't use dummies in its Network diagram. A dummy is a dependency between tasks with no work or time.

21. The Project Manager for the hotel development project is utilizing a Responsibility Assignment Matrix (RAM) to help make project execution go easier. What will this do for the Project Manager?

Correct Answer: (D) Shows who is to perform work in certain areas of the project
Explanation: The Responsibility Assignment Matrix (RAM) shows who is to perform certain work on the project. It could show who has signoff authority, has primary responsibility, or is on the team in that area. The resource list or organization chart shows who is on the project. The Network diagram shows the order of the tasks. The other answer is noise.

22. The Project Manager has been negotiating with an integrated circuit vendor for the last six months. The vendor received the Statement of Work and has responded with a proposal using fixed fee pricing. The Project Manager answers back with a letter of intent. Why did the Project Manager send this letter?

Correct Answer: (B) The Project Manager plans to buy from the vendor.
Explanation: A letter of intent is a document that declares that the buyer intends to hire or buy from the seller for a specific project. The other answers are noise.

23. The project is in a Projectized environment. There are significant challenges with meeting the tight schedule of the project and personnel leaving the company. Project personnel have been complaining to senior management about the environment hoping for a resolution. In this type of environment, who controls the resources?

Correct Answer: (A) Project Manager
Explanation: In a Projectized environment, the Project Manager traditionally controls the resources. The Project Manager has those resources available for project work as necessary. Senior management helps resolve resource conflicts. The Project Coordinator is noise.

24. A Project Manager has completed the scope statement of the project. The customer and Sponsor have shortened the schedule by four weeks and decided that the work breakdown structure will be excluded. The Project Manager informs the customer and Sponsor that this process creates the Work Breakdown Structure (WBS) for their project. Which answer best explains why the WBS is so important to a project?

Correct Answer: (D) It is used for estimating activities, cost, and resources.
Explanation: The WBS is used to help establish activities, cost and resources for project. The WBS is used for planning and controlling on the project. Budgets, staffing, and schedules are derived from the WBS, along with the deliverables. All other answers describe benefits of using a WBS.

25. The team is testing the work of the project and is having issues with a particular requirement showing the desired data. Which of the following can they use to isolate the problem?

Correct Answer: (A) Ishikawa Diagram
Explanation: Ishikawa diagrams are used in performing quality control to isolate problems. Cost-Benefit Analysis, Flowcharts, and Design of Experiments are tools used in the Plan Quality process according to the *PMBOK® Guide* - Fourth Edition.

26. The buyer has requested that the seller of services for a credit card processing project sign a fixed price contract. Fixed price contracts are also known as which of the following?

Correct Answer: (A) Lump Sum
Explanation: A fixed price contract is also known as a lump sum contract. This involves the seller providing the services for a set price. The cost plus contract pays the seller for expenses and a negotiated fee. A purchase order is a unilateral purchasing mechanism to purchase commodity type items. Time and materials contracts are typically for smaller durations or staff augmentation.

27. The Project Manager is creating planning documentation that will align the cost tracking with the Work Breakdown Structure (WBS) and the organizational chart. What is the Project Manager creating?

Correct Answer: (A) Chart of accounts
Explanation: Chart of Accounts is used to align project costs with the WBS and Organizational Structure on the project. Work packages are the lowest level of decomposition of the Work Breakdown Structure.

28. Which of the following fits the description of the person who will pay for the work and possibly own it when it is complete?

Correct Answer: (B) Customer
Explanation: The customer is the best description of the Sponsor, as they pay for the work of the project and can own it when it is complete. Senior management, Product manager and CIO are all names of what could be the sponsor, but not necessarily on every project.

29. The Project Manager has defined the risks for the project, performed probability and impact analysis and assigned risk owners to the risks. As the project management plan evolves, where will this information end up?

Correct Answer: (D) Risk register
Explanation: The risk list and risk triggers are being created in this situation. The risk list and triggers end up in the Risk Register. Risk responses end up in the Risk Register after they are created in Plan Risk Responses.

30. The Project Manager and team are planning an Internet search engine software project. They are discussing what could go differently than anticipated on the project. They are also trying to identify indicators that could warn them of potential issues. What are these indicators called?

Correct Answer: (A) Triggers
Explanation: A trigger is an indicator that a risk event could be getting ready to happen. There is no assurance that, after a trigger happens, a risk event is imminent, but it could be happening soon. Risks are factors that happen on a project and have some degree of uncertainty about them. Risk analysis and Problem solving are noise.

31. You are a Project Manager of a home remodeling project. The Budget At Completion (BAC) for this project is $68,000 US. By looking at your schedule, you should be 65% complete, but you are only 50% done. What is your Earned Value?

Correct Answer: (C) $34,000 US
Explanation: Earned Value (EV) is calculated by multiplying the percent complete of each task by its Planned Value (PV) EV = $68,000 * 40%, EV = $34,000.

32. Leads and lags can cause delays and acceleration in a schedule. This can be helpful when the goals of the schedule change. Which of the following is the best example of a Lag?

Correct Answer: (C) The need for concrete to cure an additional day because of the weather before painting the parking lines.
Explanation: The need for concrete to cure an additional day because of the weather before painting the parking line is an example of a Lag. The other three answers are noise.

33. The Project Manager is involved in decomposition of the scope of the project. Which of the following will they create as a result of this?

Correct Answer: (C) Work breakdown structure
Explanation: The Work Breakdown Structure is used in scope management to breakdown the work of the project into work packages. Bill of Materials (BOM) is used in Procurement. Risk Breakdown Structure is used in Risk. Resource Breakdown Structure is used in Human Resources.

34. Which of the following is created as a result of initiating a road expansion project?

    Correct Answer: (B) Assignment of the Project Manager
    Explanation: As a result of the charter's creation, the Project Manager is assigned to the project. Work results come from project execution. Corrective action comes from controlling. A signed contract is noise.

35. Ranking risks is performed in which of the following?

    Correct Answer: (A) Perform Qualitative Risk Analysis
    Explanation: Perform Qualitative Risk Analysis uses a risk rating matrix to rank risks and create an overall risk rating for the project. Expected Monetary Value (EMV) is used in Perform Quantitative Risk Analysis. Workarounds are done when risk events don't work. Risk triggers are indicators that a risk event could happen.

36. The Project Manager is adding people to her staff for the satellite television project. She is presently discussing salary, working hours, location, and benefits. What is the key tool she is utilizing?

    Correct Answer: (B) Negotiations
    Explanation: Negotiation is key in acquiring staff for a project. It can include salary, benefits, and job responsibilities. A Staffing Management Plan defines the staffing rules for the project. The Project Team Directory shows who is on the team. The organizational chart shows reporting structures on the project.

37. The company has been plagued by disorganized projects that are not in alignment with business goals, and not focused on interactivity between the projects where applicable. They want to have a better focus on grouping related projects together by business unit and product lines to help maximize efficiency and profitability. Which of the following best describes what they are trying to accomplish?

    Correct Answer: (B) Portfolio Management
    Explanation: Portfolio Management focuses on aligning project by business unit or product line where there is some common overlap and subject matter expertise in the area of the projects. Project Management involves creating products via projects. Operations Management involves the day-to-day repetitive tasks of a business. Management By Objectives is a goal setting technique.

38. The Internet marketing project is evaluating the size of their market, time limitations for product life cycle, revenue potential, and number of people available for the project. These are examples of what?

    Correct Answer: (B) Constraints
    Explanation: Constraints are variables that can limit the options available for the project. Constraints typically deal with resources, time, or money. Assumptions are educated guesses made on the project about items that are not known. The other two answers are noise.

39. The project is going through Quality Control. What will the Project Manager use to compare what was created to what was planned?

    Correct Answer: (B) Inspection
    Explanation: Inspection is a key tool in Quality Control. It provides validation that the product was built as intended. Checklists help establish process repeatability. Rework comes when products are not built correctly. Acceptance decisions deal with defining what is and isn't acceptable.

40. All the following are needed for creating the Scope Management Plan except...

    Correct Answer: (D) Work Breakdown Structure
    Explanation: The Work Breakdown Structure is created in the Create WBS process, which follows Collect Requirements and Define Scope. The other three answers are inputs to the Collect Requirements process which results in the Scope Management Plan.

41. A Project Manager has completed the Collect Requirements process. The customer has shortened the schedule by six weeks and decided that the Work Breakdown Structure (WBS) be modified. The Project Manager informs the customer that, by modifying the WBS, the project could be subjected to many problems. Which of the following would not be considered a problem of modifying the WBS?

    Correct Answer: (D) Project justification and objectives are not defined.
    Explanation: Project justification and objectives are part of the project Scope Statement. The Scope Statement is the output of the scope definition and would have been defined before creating the WBS. Without a defined WBS constant changes to the project, unforeseen project delays, and a poorly defined budget will always be present because the work has not been broken down into work packages.

42. A risk register that is part of the Project Management Plan on a project would be viewed as what type of communication?

    Correct Answer: (D) Formal Written
    Explanation: Any documentation associated with the contract or Project Management documentation would be considered Formal Written.

43. Your company is evaluating two projects for consideration. Project A has a 40% probability of a $3,000 US loss and a 60% probability of a $20,000 US gain. Project B has a 30% probability of a $5,000 US loss and a 70% probability of a $15,000 US gain. Which of the projects would you select based on the greatest expected monetary value?

    Correct Answer: (A) Project A
    Explanation: To calculate the Expected Monetary Value (EMV), multiply each probability by its dollar amount and add the products of the multiplications. The results are a value of $10,800 US for Project A and $9000 US for Project B. Project A would be selected with the highest Expected Monetary Value (EMV).

44. The customer has requested a five-week delay on the project while the company has winter holiday. This delay was not planned, but the union forced the issue. The company has limited resources. What is the best way to make up the five-week slip?

    Correct Answer: (C) Fast tracking
    Explanation: Fast tracking is the best option listed because it re-sequences activities to attain compression of the schedule. Crashing adds resources that aren't an option based on the question. Perform integrated change control is noise.

45. A contract is a legal agreement between a buyer and seller. There are five components of a contract. Capacity and Consideration are two of five components. All the following would be needed to have a legal contract except...

    Correct Answer: (B) Negotiation
    Explanation: Negotiation involves clarifications and mutual agreement on the requirements of the contract prior to the signing of the contract.

46. The Crosswind network studio has recently been awarded a large contract to create a new children's television show. This will require the company to move into a new office complete with production facilities 300% larger than what it presently has. The schedule is tight for this new project, and there can be no delay. The new facility is behind schedule with the studio and production facilities on pace to finish four months late. The company is attempting to validate data. If this delay proves imminent, it plans to move in temporarily with a partner of theirs with the infrastructure that will meet its needs until the building is complete. This is an example of what type of risk response?

Correct Answer: (D) Avoid
Explanation: Risk avoidance involves doing what can be done to eliminate the risk. In this case, moving to a building that would meet the company's needs will avoid the risk. Risk acceptance involves simply dealing with the risk if it happens. Mitigation is done in an attempt to minimize the bad risk. Transference is done to assign or transfer the risk to someone else.

47. Crosswind Custom Homes is building a customer's dream house. However, the electrical contractor is unavailable because they are attending a trade show in Las Vegas. This causes a delay in the completion of the house. This is an example of what?

Correct Answer: (B) External dependencies
Explanation: An External Dependency is a dependency that is outside the control of the internal organization. Mandatory is required, but internal to the organization. Crashing and Lag are noise.

48. A project you have been managing is significantly behind schedule. You have received approval to crash the project by adding three resources. The cost you have negotiated is $80 US per hour per resource. The resources will work on the schedule until it is back on track, then the contract will end. What type of contract is this?

Correct Answer: (C) Time and Materials
Explanation: A Time and Materials contract (T&M) is typically used for smaller projects or staff augmentation, such as this scenario. Under a Fixed Price contract, a seller performs work for a set price. The Cost Plus contract pays a seller costs plus a negotiated fee. The Purchase Order is used for commodity items such as those that can be mass-produced.

49. The team is involved in determining what is needed to have the quality process capture the intended results of the testing of the product. This is known as what?

Correct Answer: (B) Quality Assurance
Explanation: Quality Assurance involves ensuring that the quality plan will achieve the desired results of the project. Defining the quality rules as they relate to the project is done in Plan Quality. Measuring the output of the project is Quality Control.

50. Your DVD training project is almost complete. You have outsourced the DVD creation to an out-of-state company to complete. As the project closes down, what will be completed last?

Correct Answer: (A) Release of resources
Explanation: Release of resources is part of closing the project and occurs at the end of the process. Closing the project occurs after Close Procurements. The other answer is noise.

51. The Project Manager is hosting her first bidder's conference. Which of the following should she be sure to not be involved in at the bidder's conference?

Correct Answer: (D) Opportunity for vendors to inquire about the bids of other sellers
Explanation: Giving any vendor an opportunity to inquire about the bids of other sellers would give an unfair advantage to that vendor.

52. You are the Project Manager working with the customer on a construction project. You are required to purchase and integrate a wireless communication system throughout the construction. A contract is signed with a vendor and work has begun. Half way through the project, the customer decides to upgrade the equipment. This change will require changes to the signed contract. Who has the authority to change the contract?

Correct Answer: (C) Contract Administrator
Explanation: The Contract Administrator's main responsibility is to protect the integrity and purpose of the contract. The Contract Administrator has the authority to change the contract. The Sponsor provides the financial resources for the project. The Project Manager helps to ensure that the contract is executed successfully. The customer can request the changes, but the Contract Administrator must integrate these into the contract.

53. The project has had some challenges with personnel contribution on the project. The Project Manager feels the team isn't motivated and constantly has to tell them what to do and make sure that the team stays focused. This is an example of what?

Correct Answer: (D) Theory X environment
Explanation: In a Theory X environment, employees typically are told what to do, distrust management, and lack motivation. Theory Y is the opposite. The other two answers are noise.

54. You are the chief Project Manager of the PMO with your company. Your job is to analyze projects when they close and validate the effectiveness of the project effort. The project closing could be the result of when a project is complete or by any other means. When would you expect to close a project?

Correct Answer: (B) All the answers
Explanation: Whenever a project ends, closing the project should be completed. This allows the team and organization to learn from what worked on the project and what did not, and formally closes out the initiative.

55. The mortgage company is building an application processing center for its new home equity division. Given that this is its first venture utilizing this new type of business, a number of new processes have been created to ensure compliance with various regulatory issues. Which of the following would help verify that these processes are being accomplished?

Correct Answer: (D) Checklist
Explanation: A checklist is used to verify that a set of required steps have been performed. The process flow helps define how the company employees on the phone with customers manage the customer. A Control Chart shows output over time. A Quality Audit is done to ensure that the quality standards of the project will be met.

56. The team is in the process of determining what the customer needs for the office update project, focusing on discovering and procuring products based on the customer-defined requirements. What is this called?

Correct Answer: (C) Definition of quality
Explanation: The PMI definition of quality is "The degree to which a set of inherent characteristics fulfill requirements" (*PMBOK® Guide - Fourth Edition*).

57. Task A is worth $500, is 80% complete, and actually cost $500. Task B is worth $450, is 75% complete, and actually cost $402 so far. Task C is worth $600, is 90% complete, and has cost $550 so far. The total budget is $3000. What is the cost performance index for the tasks listed?

    Correct Answer: (C) 0.88
    Explanation: The Earned Value (EV) and Actual Cost (AC) must be calculated first. To perform this calculation, multiply the percent complete of each task by its Planned Value (PV), thereby providing the EV for each task. Sum the Actual Cost of each task to determine the total Actual Cost. Sum the Earned Value of each task to determine the total Earned Value. Then divide the Earned Value of $1277.5 by the Actual Cost of $1452. This result provides a CPI of 0.88, indicating that the project is getting $0.88 for every dollar it is spending.

58. You are a Project Manager starting negotiations with a vendor. As the vendor is attempting to maximize the value of the contract they are negotiating all the following are negotiation strategies they could use except...

    Correct Answer: (A) Force Majeure
    Explanation: Force Majeure is an act of God such as flood or tornado. Deadline implies that the negotiations must finish before a given time or the deal is off. Withdrawal implies that you are beginning to lose interest. Lying is not telling the truth.

59. You are doing some analysis associated with project selection. There is a lot of debate concerning which projects to select. You have the following to choose from: Project A with an Internal Rate of Return (IRR) of 18.2%, Project B with an Internal Rate of Return (IRR) of 21%, Project C with an Internal Rate of Return (IRR) of 13%, and Project D with an Internal Rate of Return (IRR) of 9%. If you can select only one project, which do you choose?

    Correct Answer: (B) Project B
    Explanation: With Internal Rate of Return (IRR) for a project selection technique you select the biggest percentage. In this case, Project B has the Internal Rate of Return (IRR) of 21%.

60. John has been assigned to watch for certain events associated with his area of expertise on the project and was told to implement responses from the risk register if any of these events occur. Which of the following roles is John performing on the project?

    Correct Answer: (D) Risk Owner
    Explanation: The Risk Owner is responsible for implementing Risk Response plans if the risk they are responsible for occurs. The Risk Seeker is an aggressive personality toward risk. The Project Manager and Team Lead wouldn't act unless they were the Risk Owners.

61. Which of the following best describes the lowest level of decomposition for the Work Breakdown Structure (WBS)?

    Correct Answer: (C) Breaking down work where the bottom levels of the WBS represent work packages
    Explanation: Breaking down work where it's a 4 to 80 hour work package or activity is the heuristics for WBS decomposition. The other answers verify the correctness of the decomposition.

62. The contract administrator is involved in determining the state of a contract that is nearing closure. In what process group is the Contract Administrator working?

    Correct Answer: (D) Monitoring and Controlling
    Explanation: Administer Procurements occurs in the Monitoring and Controlling process group.

63. Crosswind Custom Homes is building a customer's dream house. However, rain has delayed the finish by two weeks. The Project Manager is evaluating options to make up the lost time. After discussing the various options with Senior Management, the Project Manager has decided to fast track the project. By doing so, the Project Manager could be adding what to the project?

Correct Answer: (B) Risk

Explanation: By executing two or more tasks at once, the Project Manager introduces more risk into the project. Time change is not valid because the Project Manager is trying to recover the rain delay. Scope change is not valid because the Scope never changed. Responsibility is noise because the Project Manager is still responsible for this project.

64. Calculate the variance for the following: Pessimistic=50, Optimistic=10, Realistic=24.

Correct Answer: (D) 44.44

Explanation: The formula for variance is Pessimistic-Optimistic divided by 6, squared. The answer is $((50-10)/6)^2 = 44.44$.

65. A movie theatre construction project is going relatively well, but the people doing work on the project are complaining about reporting to two different people, each with conflicting agendas. This is an example of what type of project environment?

Correct Answer: (B) Matrix

Explanation: In a Matrix Organization, there is a functional supervisor for the employee and a Project Manager/Coordinator. The functional supervisor has daily operational activities that the employee needs to perform. The Project Manager has project activities that are expected of the employee. This is the point where the conflict occurs. The Functional Organization is organized by "silos" of departments such as accounting and marketing. A Projectized environment focuses on the team being together for the work of the project. Tight environment is noise.

66. The advertising agency has been awarded a $54M US, 8-year contract to manage the advertising campaigns of a fast food chicken restaurant. The company realizes that this work is going to require a specific skill set for 40 people. Their current workforce only has seven people with this skill set. This skill set is somewhat rare and specialized in the area they are located. They have chosen to buy a company much smaller than they are, but this company's core focus is this type of skill set. The company employs 50 people with this skill set. This is an example of what type of risk response strategy?

Correct Answer: (C) Exploit

Explanation: Exploiting the risk is to do things to grow or expand the positive aspects of the risk. Sharing the risk is to work with someone else to maximize the risk. Mitigate attempts to minimize the bad impact of the risk. Accepting the risk is to tolerate whatever happened.

67. The Project Management team has just completed the process of creating risk categories for the risks on the road construction project and is displaying the risks in a graphical format to help team members have a better understanding of what could happen on the project. They have identified among other things regulatory, supplies, labor, external and internal areas where they could have issues. What have they created?

Correct Answer: (B) Risk Breakdown Structure

Explanation: The Risk Breakdown Structure (RBS) is a graphical representation of the risk categorization and risks within those categories of the project. The Risk Management Plan is the management approach to risk on the project. The risk register contains risk lists, analysis, responses and risk owners for the project. Prioritized list of quantified risks would come in the Risk Register and involves risk ranking, not identification categorization.

68. In the communication model who is responsible if the message is delivered in a confusing and misinterpreted way?

Correct Answer: (D) Sender
Explanation: The sender is responsible for verifying that the message is clear and able to be understood. The receiver acknowledges that it was received and interpreted correctly. This typically comes from feedback provided by the receiver.

69. What is the most accurate benefit below for using a work authorization system?

Correct Answer: (D) To help ensure that work is done in the appropriate sequence
Explanation: A Work Authorization System helps ensure that certain work is done at a certain time in a certain order. This will help minimize the opportunity for Gold Plating on a project. The Work Breakdown Structure (WBS) shows what work is to be done on the project. The Responsibility Assignment Matrix (RAM) shows who is responsible for what work. "To serve as a time-tracking system" is noise.

70. The project planning is progressing on budget. The Project Manager and the team meet regularly and are ready to begin updating the project planning documents with a major scope change. What input into the planning process will help the team the most?

Correct Answer: (A) WBS
Explanation: The WBS identifies work that will require time, cost or resource. The Network diagram shows the project's activities and logical relationships. Project Management Plan is noise because Cost is part of the project management plan.

71. The Project Manager is creating an estimate for raised flooring in a data center. The project has six different bids from six vendors. Two of the bids are $4.00/sq. ft higher than the Project Manager would like to pay. Two of the other bids are $0.25 higher, but fall within the project's cost range of plus or minus 10%. Which of the following types of estimates is the Project Manager using?

Correct Answer: (C) Parametric
Explanation: Parametric is an estimating technique that uses parameters, such as so much cost per unit ($/sq. ft). The analogous estimate is also considered a top down estimate. It can be quickly created because it is based on expert knowledge of an area from previous projects. A bottom up estimate is created by the team and can take time to create because of the details. Gut feel is noise.

72. You are in the process of defining the quality standards for the clothing catalog project. You have defined the variables to measure regarding the catalog and determined what attributes are required to achieve the impact your marketing plan has defined. Which of the following is not an attribute?

Correct Answer: (A) Depth
Explanation: Depth is a variable. A variable is something that you want to measure. An attribute is the specific characteristic being evaluated. The other three answers are attributes.

73. The team is involved in Plan Risk Management. They are trying to establish an overall project risk ranking for the project. This will allow them to evaluate the project compared to others in the portfolio they are managing. What process did they just complete?

Correct Answer: (A) Perform Qualitative Risk Analysis
Explanation: Perform Qualitative Risk Analysis produces a risk ranking matrix. Identify Risks results in the discovery of risks and triggers as well as the risk register. Monitor and Control Risks results in corrective action from implementing risk response plans and workarounds as required. Mitigation is an attempt to influence the negative impact of the risk.

74. The airline reservation project has been relatively stable. The Cost Performance Index is presently 0.91 and the schedule performance index is 0.87. Risk could have been managed better from the start of this project. 60% through the execution of the project management plan, the Project Manager assigned a person to do nothing but monitor for risks and work with the people who will implement the risk response plans. What are these people called?

Correct Answer: (D) Risk Owners
Explanation: The Risk Owners are the people responsible for implementing the Risk Response Plans if the risk events occur. The Project Manager and Sponsor wouldn't be Risk Owners unless the risk response plan defined them as owners. Risk-Averse is a conservative mentality toward risk.

75. Calculate expected monetary value of the following: 0.4 probability of $5000 US, 0.3 probability of $3800 US, 0.2 probability of -$2700 US, 0.1 probability of $3000 US.

Correct Answer: (C) $2900 US
Explanation: To calculate the expected monetary value (EMV), multiply each probability by its dollar amount and add the products of the multiplications. The result is a value of $2900.

76. **Ca**lculate the PERT estimate for the following: Pessimistic=50, Optimistic=10, Realistic=24.

Correct Answer: (B) 26
Explanation: The PERT formula is Pessimistic + Optimistic+ (4*Realistic) divided by 6. The answer is (50+10+(4*24))/6 = 26.

77. What organization could audit projects in an organization to help ensure the health of the project and offer suggestions for improvement if needed?

Correct Answer: (D) Project Management Office
Explanation: The Project Management Office (PMO) can define standards, audit projects, and help mentor Project Managers or perform any other activity needed, within reason, for the management of projects within an organization.

78. Task A is worth $500, is 80% complete, and actually cost $500. Task B is worth $450, is 75% complete, and actually cost $402 so far. Task C is worth $600, is 90% complete, and has cost $550 so far. The total budget is $3000. What is the Variance at Completion for the tasks listed?

Correct Answer: (A) -$409.09
Explanation: The Variance at Completion is the difference between the Budget at Completion (BAC) and the Estimate at Completion (EAC). To calculate this value, subtract EAC ($3409.09) from BAC ($3000) for a difference of -$409.09 (VAC).

79. Crosswind Custom Development is building a customer's network infrastructure. However, a shipping delay will cause the equipment to arrive three weeks late. The Project Manager evaluates the schedule and determines that by crashing the project, it could be placed back on schedule by compressing the deployment of the equipment. After discussing this with senior management, the Project Manager has decided to crash the project. By doing so, the Project Manager is adding what to the project?

Correct Answer: (D) Cost change
Explanation: By adding more resources to the project, the cost will increase. Time change is not valid because the Project Manager is trying to recover the time due to the shipping delay. Scope change is not valid because the Scope never changed. Responsibility is noise because the Project Manager is still responsible for this project.

80. You are a Project Manager trying to estimate the duration of a project. You would like to use an Activity on Arrow diagram as your Network diagram. You decide to use an estimating method with three activities: Optimistic, Pessimistic, and Most Holistic. What estimating method would you use?

Correct Answer: (D) None of the above
Explanation: Optimistic and Pessimistic are two of the three estimates used for PERT. The other needed is most likely (or Realistic) which is missing; therefore, you have only two estimates. CPM uses a one-time estimate per task. GERT uses a feedback loop. PERT uses Optimistic, Pessimistic, and Most Likely/Realistic estimates per activity.

81. The project team has just started planning as a result of the charter being signed. The charter provides all the following except...

Correct Answer: (A) Defines the Scope Statement
Explanation: The Scope Statement is an output from the Collect Requirements process. The other answers are included in the charter.

82. Which of the following would a team create as a result of using a Change Control System?

Correct Answer: (B) Approved changes
Explanation: Approved changes are the output of a Change Control System. These are change requests that have gone into the system and been approved. Change requests involve a desired change that hasn't been approved yet. Impact analysis involves identifying what impact the change might have on the project or environment. Signoff involves receiving approval. In this case, signoff is noise.

83. The project team is planning an upgrade to a client's movie production studio. During planning, the team members discover that the lab where the editing processes are to reside will not have sufficient space, forcing the client to lease another building. This building will also be shared with another department. What type of Cost would this be?

Correct Answer: (B) Indirect
Explanation: Indirect costs are costs incurred for the benefit of one or more project or departments. Direct costs are directly attributable to the project and spent only on the project work. Variable costs are costs that fluctuate with what is produced. Indirect Fixed is noise.

84. The project is going well until a Stakeholder requests a significant change based on a modification in the Stakeholder's business process. After meeting with the team to determine impact it appears that the change will likely double the length of the project because of the complexity associated with the change. The change request and its impact analysis are going before the Change Control Board (CCB) for review and potential approval. What is the purpose of the Change Control Board (CCB)?

Correct Answer: (D) To control change by approval of needed changes and rejection of unneeded changes to the project
Explanation: The purpose of a Change Control Board (CCB) is to control change via approval of only the needed changes and rejection of those changes not vital to the success of the project.

85. To develop a CDMA base station for your company, a project requires some new test equipment and a new D++ complier. The finance department explains that this is a capital purchase to be depreciated using the sum of the years digits. This is an example of what?

Correct Answer: (B) Accelerated Depreciation
Explanation: Sum of the digits and double declining balance are examples of accelerated depreciation. Standard and straight-line depreciation are the same. The Fixed Direct Cost is noise.

86. Which of the following would a Project Manager use to track cost related activities on a project?

   Correct Answer: (C) Control Costs
   Explanation: Control Costs is the process used to control costs on a project. The Cost Management Plan helps establish the cost rules for the project. The Work Breakdown Structure helps decompose the work of the project. The Budget Management Plan is noise.

87. The project planning for the trade show is progressing on schedule. The Project Manager and the team are meeting to begin cost estimating. The Sponsor has said that estimates must be very accurate. Which of the following estimating techniques will provide the most accuracy?

   Correct Answer: (A) Bottom up estimating
   Explanation: In bottom-up estimating, the Project Manager and the project team work together to create a complete estimate from the bottom up. Cost estimating is the process the Project Manager and team are executing. Analogous estimating creates a high estimate with no significant detail.

88. The advertising agency has been awarded a $20M US contract to provide consulting and support services to a restaurant chain in creating an advertising campaign. If things go well, they will get the next phase of the project that will include world wide advertising. The advertising agency is relatively small, and this contract is bigger than anything they have been awarded to date. To ensure that they can effectively complete the contract, and not jeopardize their other work they have chosen to partner with another company to do the work. This is an example of what type of risk response strategy?

   Correct Answer: (D) Share
   Explanation: Sharing the risk with another company is what is happening here. Exploiting the risk is to do things to grow or expand the positive aspects of the risk. Mitigate would attempt to minimize the bad impact of the risk. Accepting the risk would be to tolerate whatever happened.

89. The Project Manager is reviewing testing output data from the NUBUS system. Generally, the data looks good other than one issue. He observes seven consecutive data points on one side of the mean in three areas on the control chart. What is this called?

   Correct Answer: (C) A violation of the Seven Run Rule
   Explanation: The Seven Run Rule is a situation in which there are at least seven consecutive data points on one side of the mean, implying that the process could have some type of problem. The other three answers are noise

90. A marketing campaign is being built to support a new product at a utility company. The company doesn't have data on what volume to expect from the marketing campaign and the associated advertising. This data is important because it will help drive the number of employees needed department so customers' needs can be met. The Project Manager remembers that a similar project was by a company his company acquired. He begins to review data from this project. This is a best example of what?

   Correct Answer: (A) Historical Information
   Explanation: Historical Information contains the results of previous projects and performance. Lessons Learned are the reason behind the corrective action chosen and become Historical Information. Constraints are factors that limit the options available on the project. Assumptions come into play when something on the project is not known.

91. The client has requested a four-week delay on the project while the company remodels its training facilities. This delay wasn't planned, but the facilities were going to be shut down by the safety board for various violations. The company is limited with its resource options and will have to make up the work quickly. This delay will be best shown in what?

Correct Answer: (B) Network diagram
Explanation: The Network diagram shows the sequencing and length of the diagram. The Responsibility Assignment Matrix (RAM) shows who is responsible for what and doesn't include time. The WBS shows what work is in the project but doesn't focus on how long it should take. The budget deals with the costs of the project, not time.

92. The software development company has recently been awarded a large contract to create a new animation software program. This will require the company to move into a new office complete with production facilities twice their current size. The schedule is tight for this new project. The new facility is behind schedule with the cubicles and network wiring on pace to finish three weeks late. If this can't be done on time and will slip three weeks, the company has decided there is nothing it can do, and it will simply deal with the consequences. This is an example of what type of risk response?

Correct Answer: (A) Accept
Explanation: Risk Acceptance involves simply dealing with the risk if it happens. In this case, the project could fall through if the failure of the project to start on time impacts the schedule causing delays. Risk Avoidance involves doing what can be done to eliminate the risk. Mitigation is done to attempt to minimize the bad risk. Transference is done to assign or transfer the risk to someone else.

93. A Project Manager was assigned to manage a project to develop pink widgets for the Project Manager's company. The project will cost the company $510,000 over the next 12 months. It is projected that the widgets will earn the company $37,500 per month. How much time will it take to recover the cost for this project?

Correct Answer: (D) 14 months
Explanation: The Return of Investment is $37,500 per month and the cost of the project is $510,000. The amount of time to recover this investment is ($510,000 / $37,500 = 13.6 months or 14 months).

94. The development team is building a new video creation product. This is a new product type at their company, and the market for the product is volatile and changing every 3 months. According to the product manager a key to success will be the ability to evolve the planning as more information about the market is discovered, but there could be fluctuation in the direction of the development. Which type of scheduling approach best fits this need?

Correct Answer: (B) Rolling wave planning
Explanation: In an environment where there is a great degree of flexibility or instability it's good to use a rolling wave planning approach. This allows the team to plan out as much as reasonably possible, and as they are executing that part of the plan, they continue to plan future work as they learn more about it. Crashing involves putting more resources on the critical path tasks. Fast tracking involves re-sequencing already defined tasks to compress the overall duration of the schedule. Precedence diagramming is a network diagramming technique.

95. The team implemented a risk response plan when a vendor was unable to fulfill a contract commitment for a training class. The response was to choose another vendor. However, in this type of training, it's hard to find a good company, and the one selected doesn't have a much better reputation. The new company is somewhat better at meeting the terms of the contract, but still has some issues from time to time, which is no surprise. What best describes these issues?

Correct Answer: (C) Residual risk
Explanation: Residual risk is risk that can remain after a risk event has been implemented. Secondary risk involves the creation of new risk from implementing a risk response. The risk response plan shows what is done and who is responsible for doing it if a risk event occurs. The workaround is done when risk responses do not work.

96. The Project Management Team is working in the executing and monitoring/controlling phases of the project. There are four sponsors and 34 Stakeholders on the project. Which of the following is the most likely to focus on communication at this point in the project to ensure the project achieves the quality standards established in planning?

Correct Answer: (D) At key interface points where the various work packages come together
Explanation: The key interface points to where pieces of the project come together in executing. If the Project Manager fails to ensure they come together as needed, there will be problems completing the project work as intended. Planning revisions would happen in planning as a result of change control. The other answers are noise.

97. In performing management of the project, the Project Manager spends a large percentage of her time communicating. Which of the following is the best advantage of doing this on the project?

Correct Answer: (D) A greater emphasis on successful integration of the various pieces of the project
Explanation: A greater emphasis on successful integration of the various pieces of the project occurs when the Project Manager ensures successful communication between the various pieces of the project. A detailed project file is a byproduct of successful communication. An accurate Communication Management Plan helps ensure communication with the right people. A Theory Y management style is noise.

98. Which of the following would a Project Manager use to evaluate a hurricane that hit the data center on a project? The Project Manager would use which of the following to compensate for the loss from the hurricane?

Correct Answer: (C) Management Reserves
Explanation: Unknown unknowns are created for management reserves. These are factors that aren't expected to happen. Contingency reserves are created for known unknowns. These are events that we know will happen; we just don't know how much of it will happen. Schedule Reserves and Risk Management are noise.

99. The construction project is almost finished. The team is involved in many different activities to close the project. The team members are in the process of creating project archives. All the following are examples of project archives except...

Correct Answer: (C) Negotiations parameters
Explanation: Archives are created as a result of the project. They include financial records, contracts, and internal project documentation. Completed government clearance applications could be part of archives. Negotiations parameters wouldn't be part of the archives unless they were associated with other project documentation.

100. A Project Manager has decided to outsource the installation of an electrical security system in their business offices. The buyer has given specific details to the vendor on the schedule and cost of each site. This will also be a fixed price contract. What type of Scope of work is being provided to the sellers?

Correct Answer: (C) Design
Explanation: A Design Scope of Work shows specifically what is to be created. The functionality Scope of work shows the general functional specifications that the outcome of the project needs to have when complete. A Time and Materials (T&M) is a contract used for smaller projects or staff augmentation. A Scope Statement defines exactly what it is being created or accomplished by the procurement initiatives.

101. A Project Manager has completed the Define Scope process. The customer and Sponsor have shortened the schedule by eight weeks and decided that the work breakdown structure will be cut in half. What would be the best action the Project Manager should take?

Correct Answer: (B) Discuss with the customer and Sponsor the ramifications of having the WBS not reflect the true work of the project.
Explanation: The Project Manager should discuss with the customer that the value of the WBS and that the WBS is the foundation of the project. Providing the customer and Sponsor an updated schedule and budget would not be a true estimate because the WBS has not been defined completely. Beginning the execution of the project would be a possible answer, but without the WBS, the Project Manager does not have the work packages. Calling a meeting and notify notifying the team of the schedule change would be de-motivating factors because the schedule has been shortened and the team does not know what to develop.

102. A contract administrator would use all the following as contracts except…

Correct Answer: (C) Proposal
Explanation: Proposals are seller-prepared documents that describe the seller's ability and willingness to provide the requested product. It is not a contract.

103. Calculate the standard deviation for the following: Pessimistic=50, Optimistic=10, Realistic=24.

Correct Answer: (D) 6.667
Explanation: The formula for standard deviation is Pessimistic-Optimistic divided by 6.   The answer is (50-10)/6 = 6.667.

104. You are a Project Manager trying to decide what quality approach to implement at your company. You have decided that it is in the best interest of the company to do testing while in the developing phase to get immediate feedback. You also decide to include statistical analysis for evaluating the output data. This philosophy is known as…

Correct Answer: (C) Total Quality Management
Explanation: Total Quality Management uses continuous improvement as employees find ways to improve quality. Quality Assurance involves ensuring that the quality plan will achieve the desired results of the project. The Quality Management Plan describes how the project management team will implement its quality policy. ISO 9000 is a Quality System Management Standard

105. A project will be using a vendor to install computer network wiring in a three story shopping center. The buyer is asking vendors to describe how they will do this work and how much it will cost. What type of document will be used to solicit this information?

Correct Answer: (B) Request for Proposal (RFP)
Explanation: A Request for Proposal (RFP) deals with a detailed, very specific approach to a customized solution and cost. A Request for Quote (RFQ) involves getting prices from a company for goods or services. A Request for Information (RFI) deals with finding potential vendors for consideration for proposals or quotes. An Invitation for Bid (IFB) is similar to the RFP but is typically used in government contracting.

106. The Project Management Team is creating the Quality Management Plan. The Sponsor has told them to focus on not having to redo things, and to try to do things on the project that will help the project get done efficiently and increase profits from the product of the project. What best describes what the Sponsor is asking for?

Correct Answer: (C) Zero defects
Explanation: The Zero defects practice aims to reduce defects as a way to directly increase profits. The concept of Zero defects led to the development of Six Sigma in the 1980s. Total Quality Management uses continuous improvement where employees find ways to improve quality. Kaizen is the continuous, incremental improvement of an activity to create more value with less waste. Fitness for Use is to satisfy the real need of the customers and Stakeholders.

107. Which of the following would a contract administrator use if they are using a unilateral contract?

Correct Answer: (D) Purchase Order
Explanation: In a unilateral contract, with uni meaning one-sided negotiations, a Purchase Order is the answer. The other three answers are noise.

108. Which of the following can the new Project Manager use to see what the reporting relationships are on her new data cleansing project?

Correct Answer: (C) Organizational Breakdown Structure (OBS)
Explanation: The Organizational Breakdown Structure (OBS) is also known as an Organizational Chart. It shows what reporting relationships are on the project. The Staffing Management Plan defines the staffing rules as they relate to the project. The Responsibility Assignment Matrix shows who is responsible for what on the project. The Resource histogram shows what quantities of resources are utilized over time.

109. Which of the roles would control resources in a balanced matrix environment?

Correct Answer: (C) Functional management
Explanation: Functional Managers control resources and run business units. In a balanced matrix environment they are responsible for the resources and the Project Manager is responsible for the project. Senior management is responsible for a number of areas on a project. The main responsibility is to help support the project and resolve resource conflicts as they occur. For situational questions, assume that you are in a Balanced Matrix environment, unless otherwise stated. The Project Manager's responsibility is to drive the completion of project work. Typically, the Sponsor's responsibility is to pay for the project and own it when it is complete.

110. A Project Manager is assigned to a project that is in the design phase of creating a BBX transceiver. The Project Manager is in the process of reviewing work completed to gain Formal Acceptance. This is known as what?

Correct Answer: (A) Verify Scope
Explanation: Verify Scope is the process of obtaining Formal Acceptance of the project Scope by the Stakeholders. Control Scope ensures that changes are agreed upon, determines if the Scope change has occurred, and manages the actual changes. Quality Assurance and Quality Control are concerned with the correctness of the Work Results, not the acceptance of the work results.

111. The shirt printing company has added a new line for its silk screening business. It involves new technology to build printed images on the shirts quickly and cheaper. The company anticipates that this new technology will allow it to make a more efficient yield from the printing process. The company is also increasing the amount of insurance it has on its main facility because there has been flooding in the area in recent years from excessive rain. Adding this insurance is an example of what?

Correct Answer: (D) Insurable risk
Explanation: Pure risk is also known as insurable risk. This is something that you can buy insurance for such as to protect a building. Business risk is the risk associated with being in business for a profit or loss. Conformance to quality relates to a proactive mentality toward quality. ISO 9000 is a quality standard

112. Task A is worth $500, is 80% complete, and actually cost $500. Task B is worth $450, is 75% complete, and actually cost $402 so far. Task C is worth $600, is 90% complete, and has cost $550 so far. The total budget is $3000. What is the schedule variance for the tasks listed?

Correct Answer: (C) -$272.50
Explanation: The Earned Value (EV) and Planned Value (PV) must be calculated first. To perform this calculation, multiply the percent complete of each task by its Planned Value (PV), thereby providing the EV for each task. Sum the Planned Value of each task to determine the total Planned Value. Sum the Earned Value of each task to determine the total Earned Value. Then subtract the Planned Value of $1550 from Earned Value of $1277.5, thereby providing a SV of -$272.5. This means that the project is $272.5 behind schedule.

113. The Project Manager is creating an estimate for building a company workout facility. It is something that is new to the Project Manager and he wants to make sure all the work of the project is covered. He decides to create a Bottom-Up estimate. All the following are advantages of this type of estimate except...

Correct Answer: (D) It takes a great amount of time to create.
Explanation: Taking a great amount of time to create is not an advantage of the estimating. All the other answers are advantages characteristic of the Bottom-Up estimate.

114. In reviewing the benefits and challenges of a Projectized, Matrix and Functional Organization, which of the following is considered an advantage of a Functional Organization?

Correct Answer: (B) Business unit competency
Explanation: Business unit competency comes from a Functional Organization. For example, accounting expertise resides in an accounting department. The other answers are characteristic of a Project Management environment.

115. The Project Manager has scheduled weekly status meetings with the team and three customer contacts. The meetings have been disorganized with people addressing their own needs and taking longer than needed on unplanned items with no discipline. Which of the following would improve the meetings?

Correct Answer: (B) Create and publish an agenda, and establish the leader of the meeting
Explanation: Creating and publishing an agenda, and knowing who is in charge of a meeting are two ways to have a highly organized effective meeting.

116. Which of the following is not a regulation?

Correct Answer: (C) The average number of losing lottery tickets in a week
Explanation: The average number of losing lottery tickets in a week. It's not a regulation the other three answers are. The other three answers have defined criteria that they must meet to be acceptable.

117. Which of the following does the Project Manager need to create a variance report?

Correct Answer: (A) Baseline measurements
Explanation: Baseline measurements allow the Project Manager to report performance by comparing Work Results to the baseline on the project. Status reports are generally an output of this area. Status reports can lead to Change Requests. Status reports typically end up in the Project Archives.

118. You are the Project Manager on an oil pipeline project. Due to the rough terrain, the scope of the project had to be modified to compensate for the required drilling and excavating changes. You need to verify that these changes have been put in place. What would best help you determine this?

Correct Answer: (A) Project Scope Statement updates
Explanation: Project Scope Statement Updates would help provide validation that the updates to the project scope had been added to the plan and into execution if they should have been acted upon by that point in time. Control Scope System defines the procedures by which the project Scope may be changed. Scope Management Plan describes how project Scope will be managed and how Scope changes will be integrated into the project. Scope changes are any modifications to the agreed-upon project Scope as defined by the approved WBS.

119. You are the Project Manager for a consumer research database project. You have just finished putting together all the various plans into an integrated complete document that the team will use to guide them in creating the project work. What step have you just completed?

Correct Answer: (B) Developing the Project Management Plan
Explanation: The Project Management Plan is the cumulative document that contains all the project management plans including the Budget, Schedule, Scope Statement, WBS, Risk, Staffing, and other plans. Develop Schedule and Project Management Plan Execution are processes that do not fit here. The charter signoff would have occurred before the project planning had begun.

120. The Project Manager is performing risk management on a project. She is reviewing risk triggers in the Risk Register. All the following are accurate about risk triggers except...

Correct Answer: (C) A trigger is an indicator that a risk event will occur.
Explanation: A trigger is a factor which indicates that a risk event is possible. Just because a trigger occurs doesn't automatically mean that a risk event is imminent. A trigger normally wouldn't become a risk.

121. You are the Project Manager of an engineering project for a cellular base station with a one-year schedule as defined by the project management plan. You need a spectrum analyzer. During the procurement process, you have decided to rent this equipment. The rental cost is $506 per month. What type of cost is this?

Correct Answer: (C) Variable
Explanation: Variable costs fluctuate with what is produced or the amount of time something is used. Fixed costs are costs that are consistent on a project. The $506 per month will not change throughout the year. Indirect costs are costs that are incurred for the benefit of one or more projects or departments. Direct costs are directly attributable to the project and spent only on the project work.

122. In evaluating slack on a project which of the following formulas can a Project Manager use to calculate it?

    Correct Answer: (A) Late Finish-Early Finish (LF-EF)
    Explanation: Slack is calculated by subtracting either the Late Finish (LF) from the Early Finish (EF) or the Late Start (LS) from the early start (ES).

123. A project will be using a vendor to purchase broadcast cameras and computers for a call center for a television channel run by a foreign government. The government has requested a proposal from prospective sellers of the equipment. What type of document is being provided to the sellers?

    Correct Answer: (A) Invitation for Bid (IFB)
    Explanation: An Invitation for Bid (IFB) is similar to the RFP but is typically used in government contracting. A Request for Quotes (RFQ) involves getting prices from a company for goods or services. A Request for Proposal (RFP) deals with a very detailed and specific approach to a customized solution. A Request for Information (RFI) deals with finding potential vendors for consideration for proposals or quotes.

124. You are doing risk management on a project, discussing with the sponsor the probabilities of finishing the project on schedule. What must the sum of all probabilities equal?

    Correct Answer: (B) 100%
    Explanation: The sum of all probabilities must equal 100% or 1.0. The other answers involve the percentage for 1 sigma is 68.26%, 2 sigma is 95.46%, and 3 sigma is 99.73%.

125. The electronics project is going through planning to create a less costly version of an existing product. In evaluating the Triple Constraint, which of the following is the highest priority?

    Correct Answer: (D) They are all equal unless otherwise stated in the charter.
    Explanation: The Triple Constraint implies that all three components (Scope, Time, and Cost) are equal unless otherwise defined in the charter.

126. The marketing project is on schedule and under budget. The customer is pleased, but would like to add a few features. As a result, a new team is brought in to help the existing team implement this additional work. Before the team arrives, Senior Management would like to see where the project stands. Which of the following do you show them?

    Correct Answer: (D) Milestone chart
    Explanation: The Milestone Chart is used for executive reporting. It shows the target dates and status of the high level milestones. The Gantt chart shows the people doing the work where the project is working to the plan. The Network diagram is used to show the sequencing of activities on the project. The Work Breakdown Structure (WBS) is used to show the work that is in the project

127. Task A is worth $500, is 80% complete, and actually cost $500. Task B is worth $450, is 75% complete, and actually cost $402 so far. Task C is worth $600, is 90% complete, and has cost $550 so far. The total budget is $3000. What is the total Earned Value for the tasks listed?

    Correct Answer: (B) $1277.5
    Explanation: To calculate the Earned Value (EV), multiply the percent complete of each task by its Planned Value (PV), thereby providing the EV for each task. The next step is to add the Earned Value for each task to determine the total Earned Value for the project. This amount is $1277.50.

128. The Sponsor is reviewing two different projects for approval. It has determined that the company has enough resources to do only one project. Project A is worth $800,000 US and Project B is worth $1,650,000. What is the Opportunity Cost of selecting Project B?

Correct Answer: (B) $800,000 US

Explanation: The Opportunity Cost of selecting Project B is the value of what is not selected. This is the value of Project A ($800,000).

129. You are the Project Manager on the development of a RAID 4 computer storage network. The customer has been very concerned about the correctness and acceptance of the work results as they have had corrupt data in the past and the goal is to have this serve as a backup system. You are not sure what the customer is saying about the "correctness and acceptance" so you review your *PMBOK® Guide*. What areas below will likely be involved in attaining what the government is concerned about?

Correct Answer: (D) Verify Scope and Quality Control

Explanation: Verify Scope is concerned with obtaining formal acceptance of the work, and Quality Control is concerned with the correctness of the work. Control Scope ensures that changes are agreed upon, determines if the Scope change has occurred, and manages the actual changes. Quality Assurance evaluates overall project performance. Plan Quality identifies which quality standards are relevant to the project. Administrative Closure documents project results to formalize acceptance of the product of the project.

130. In evaluating a make or buy analysis of services needed all the following are reasons for outsourcing work except...

Correct Answer: (B) Labor rates in the foreign countries are comparable to your company's labor rate.

Explanation: If the labor rates are the same as your company's labor rate, there is no reason to outsource the work. The other answers are good reasons to outsource the work.

131. Task A is worth $500, is 80% complete, and actually cost $500. Task B is worth $450, is 75% complete, and actually cost $402 so far. Task C is worth $600, is 90% complete, and has cost $550 so far. The total budget is $3000. What is the cost variance for the tasks listed?

Correct Answer: (A) -$174.50

Explanation: The Earned Value (EV) and actual Cost (AC) must be calculated first. To perform this calculation, multiply the percent complete of each task by its Planned Value (PV), thereby providing the EV for each task. Sum the Actual Cost of each task to determine the total Actual Cost. Sum the Earned Value of each task to determine the total Earned Value. Then subtract the Actual Cost of $1452 from the Earned Value of $1277.5, thereby providing a CV of -$174.50. This means that the project is $174.50 over budget.

132. A Project Manager is beginning the solicitation process to find companies that can potentially provide the needed services. The buyer wants to consider only sellers of the services that have done projects of greater than $20M US and have employees with a high level security clearance. What screening mechanism is this?

Correct Answer: (D) Qualified Seller List

Explanation: A Qualified Sellers List has information on relevant past experience and other characteristics of prospective sellers. Advertising lets prospective vendors know what about the company's potential needs. Weighting System is a tool used in source selection. A Bidder Conference lets companies ask a buyer questions and get clarification on any potential issues.

133. The Project Manager is in the process of closing the project and plans a meeting with the team to document and discuss how the project went. This activity is known as what?

   Correct Answer: (A) Lessons Learned
   Explanation: Lessons Learned is the process of discussing and documenting what went good and bad on a project so they can help projects in the future run more efficiently.

134. The Sponsor on the airport runway project has just told the Project Manager, about a change he wants. He says that the change will cost 20% less and should not cause any problems to the existing environment. Which of the following should concern the Project Manager the most?

   Correct Answer: (C) Scope and Schedule impact
   Explanation: Scope and Schedule impact should be the most concerning, assuming the cost impact is true. Quality is noise.

135. A Project Manager is in the process of using a rolling wave planning approach and documenting the project work. With help for the product description, the Project Manager has defined the Scope Statement for the project. What process is the Project Manager performing?

   Correct Answer: (B) Define Scope
   Explanation: Define Scope is the process of progressively elaborating and documenting the project work. Control Scope ensures that changes are agreed upon, determines if the Scope change has occurred, and manages the actual changes. Verify Scope is the process of obtaining Formal Acceptance of the project Scope by the Stakeholders. Collect Requirements involves creating the Scope Management Plan for the project.

136. Home Creation store is starting to use Just in Time inventory because its inventory costs are greater than the industry average. The company feels this policy will help minimize inventory costs and be more efficient. What is the amount of inventory needed for this type of process?

   Correct Answer: (C) Zero
   Explanation: The amount of inventory needed for Just in Time (JIT) inventory is optimally zero days, implying that inventory arrives when needed.

137. The project team is working together on the airport runway addition project. The Project Manager has delivered a report that describes how much work should have been accomplished, how much work is actually accomplished, and the actual cost to complete the work. The Project Manager plans to use this report to show the state of the schedule and budget. What type of report is this?

   Correct Answer: (D) Earned Value report
   Explanation: The Earned Value report focuses on Earned Value measurement. It focuses on Actual Cost (AC), Earned Value (EV), Planned Value (PV), and a number of measurements that can come from that. The Progress report shows what has been done in a certain time period on the project. The Status report shows what has been completed to date on the project. The Variance report shows the difference between what is happening on the project and what should have happened.

138. You are in the initial phase of a project and are doing an estimate for a project that requires a MRI lab for a hospital to be built. What is the estimate range you would use for this project?

Correct Answer: (B) -25% to +75%
Explanation: The range of an Order Of Magnitude (OOM) estimate is -25% to +75% and is used during the Initiation phase of a project. The Budget estimate has a range of -10% to +25%. The Definitive estimate has a range of -5% to +10%. The -25% to +85% is noise.

139. The project team has begun development on a project in a new market for their company. Because the market is so unstable, the product they are creating doesn't necessarily have all the details defined before planning begins. The team has to plan as much as possible and begin the work. As they learn more about the work, they will adapt their planning. Which of the following best describes the approach?

Correct Answer: (A) Progressive elaboration
Explanation: Progressive elaboration is used when not all the details are known about the project. The team begins planning and executing while continuing to plan as they learn more about the project. Extreme programming is a form of progressive elaboration, but not covered on the exam. Project management is doing projects to create products. Total Quality Management is a proactive approach to quality on the project.

140. The quality improvement project is doing procurement audits. It is identifying successes and failures of the procurement process. This identification is important for Formal Acceptance and Closure. What process is the project in?

Correct Answer: (C) Close Procurements
Explanation: Close Procurements uses procurement audits to determine the successes and failures of the procurement process. Closing the project is done in the closing process and is performed when the project or phase stops. Quality Assurance validates the quality standards defined for the project. In Closing, the project finishes.

141. The Crosswind broadcasting has recently been awarded a large contract to create a new children's television show. This will require the company to move into a new office complete with production facilities 300% larger than what it presently has. The schedule is tight for this new project, and there can be no delay. The new facility is behind schedule with the sets and production facilities on pace to finish two months late. The company is trying to use an incentive fee to motivate the provider of these services to complete the work as quickly as possible even if it results in a smaller delay. This is an example of what type of risk response?

Correct Answer: (B) Mitigate
Explanation: Risk mitigation is done in an attempt to minimize the bad risk. In this case, management is attempting to minimize the impact of a schedule delay. Risk acceptance involves simply dealing with the risk if it happens. Risk avoidance involves doing what can be done to eliminate the risk. Transference is done to assign or transfer the risk to someone else.

142. You are the Project Manager for a national satellite rollout project. You are required to purchase and integrate reporting software for all the retail stores. As the Project Manager, you want one price from the vendors for the purchase and implementation of this product. What type of document should be used?

Correct Answer: (C) Request for Proposal
Explanation: A Request for Proposal (RFP) deals with a detailed, very specific approach to a customized solution and a total price. An Invitation For Bid (IFB) is a sealed bidding process that lists seller's firm price to complete the detail work. This is typically used in government bidding. A Request for Information (RFI) deals with finding potential vendors for consideration for proposals or quotes. A Request for Quote (RFQ) involves getting prices from a company for goods or services.

143. You are testing what the team has created on the project. You are trying to determine if a project is producing a low quality or low-grade product. Which statement best describes the differences?

Correct Answer: (D) Low quality is always a problem, but low grade may not.
Explanation: Low quality is always a problem on a project, and low grade may be acceptable to the customer. Products can have high quality but low grade in which a product does not have bugs but has low grade because of the limited features. Products can have low quality, but high grade in which a product can have many bugs with numerous features. Low quality may not be a problem, but low grade is always a problem is inaccurate. In this case, low quality is always a problem.

144. The project management plan contains all the following except…

Correct Answer: (D) Corrective action
Explanation: Corrective action occurs throughout the project as changes are needed to improve/modify the plan or work results. The schedule is required to complete the project management plan. The Staffing Management Plan is used to develop the staffing needs of the project. The Change Control System is usually defined in the plan.

145. The Project Manager is creating an estimate for an electrical sub-system that is being built. The customer is now creating his budget for the next two calendar years and needs this estimate as soon as possible. A Senior Project Manager has managed many projects that included building sub-systems and is considered an expert. You solicit his help on the estimate. Which of the following types of estimates is the Project Manager using?

Correct Answer: (B) Analogous
Explanation: The Analogous estimate is also considered a top down estimate. It can be quickly created because it is based on expert knowledge of an area from previous projects. Parametric is an estimating technique that uses parameters such as so much cost per unit ($/sq. ft). Created by the team, a Bottom-Up estimate can take time to create because of the details. Delphi Technique is a method to obtain expert opinions. It is not an estimate tool.

146. The project has five people on it. Four more are added. What is the total number of communication channels added to the project?

Correct Answer: (D) 26 Channels
Explanation: To calculate this value, calculate the number of communication channels with five people. The formula is $N*(N-1)/2$. This means that, with five people, there are 10 channels of communication. Next, add the four additional people for a total of nine people and use the communication channel formula. This shows that there are 36 communication channels with nine people on the project. Subtract 36 from 10 for a difference, the answer of 26 communication channels.

147. The Project Manager and team have completed the project Scope within budget, but behind schedule, and have just received signoff from the customer. What is this activity called?

Correct Answer: (A) Formal Acceptance
Explanation: Verify Scope helps lead to Formal Acceptance. Contract closeout occurs when closing out a contract with a vendor. Project archives are created when a project is closed out.

148. The company is in the testing phase of its software project, tracking defects that come in from premium customers who are testing the beta version of the project work. Given the nature of a new project, a variety of defects is being discovered over time. Which of the following will the team use to evaluate this data graphically?

Correct Answer: (C) Run Chart

Explanation: A run chart gives a picture of the process output over time. The Pareto diagram shows frequency of defects in a graphical format. The flowchart shows process flow. Fishbone diagram shows what problems could happen or might be happening.

149. According to the *PMBOK®* Guide - Fourth Edition, where does Estimate Activity Resources occur?

Correct Answer: (C) Time

Explanation: The Estimate Activity Resources is a major process of Time. It determines what resources and what quantities of each should be used.

150. The team is involved in creating the Project Management Plan. They are in the process of evaluating risks that could occur on the project. Which of the following best describes project risk?

Correct Answer: (A) It can be either a negative or positive event.

Explanation: Risk can be of negative or positive consequence on a project. It is something that can happen but hasn't yet. Because risk involves uncertainty, it involves what could happen, not what has happened.